JOE FONG

JANE PARKS-McKAY

THE MAKE-OVER

A TEEN'S GUIDE TO LOOKING & FEELING BEAUTIFUL

illustrated by Betty de Araujo

William Morrow & Company, Inc. | New York

To Tessie and Mrs. Brown—my first two students.
I will always love you.

The personality evaluation sections on pages 9–15 are reprinted by permission of A & W Publishers, Inc. from *Values Clarification: A Handbook of Practical Strategies for Teachers and Students,* New Revised Edition by Sidney B. Simon, Leland W. Howe, and Howard Kirschenbaum. Copyright © 1972; Copyright © 1978. Hart Publishing Company, Inc.

PHOTO CREDITS:
Aro Photographics, Los Gatos, Calif., p. 2; The Portrait Gallery, Los Gatos, Calif., p. 3.

Library of Congress Cataloging in Publication Data
Parks-McKay, Jane.   The make-over: a teen's guide to looking and feeling beautiful. Includes index. Summary: Includes advice on grooming, diet, make-up, exercise, wardrobe planning, nutrition, and behavior. 1. Beauty, Personal—Juvenile literature. 2. Youth—Health and hygiene—Juvenile literature. 3. Clothing and dress—Juvenile literature. 4. Cosmetics—Juvenile literature. 5. Hairdressing—Juvenile literature. 6. Exercise—Juvenile literature. 7. Hand—Care and hygiene—Juvenile literature. [1. Beauty, Personal. 2. Grooming] I. de Araujo, Betty, ill. II. Title.
RA777.P34   1985   646.7'042   84-29557
ISBN 0-688-04155-8
ISBN 0-688-04156-6 (pbk.)

ACKNOWLEDGMENTS

Nineteen years ago, I had two dreams. One was to become a teacher, teaching others how to become the best they could be. That dream became a reality eleven years ago. My second dream was to write a beauty book, so that others could learn what I had learned. After seven years in the making, that dream has now become a reality, too.

A project like this one is not a solitary effort, to be sure. And none of it would have happened without the help of many people who have not only supported me in my image consulting and modeling business, but in writing this book, as well. It is here that I wish to acknowledge these wonderful people. My deepest thanks, then, go to

- Andrea Curley, my editor at William Morrow, a joy to work with, and I appreciate all of her many fine suggestions, the time she's put into the project, and above all, her belief in me.
- Barbara Kouts, of the Spitzer Agency in New York, my patient and very hard-working literary agent, who nurtured my dream. This book would not have gotten this far without her.
- Dr. Jean Poulos, my nutritionist in Santa Cruz, California, who spent her valuable time proofing the figure chapter.
- Dr. Anthony G. Matukas, my dermatologist who not only proofed various parts of the manuscript, but has also patiently answered my countless medical questions over the years.
- Dr. Lowell S. Birch, my knowledgeable chiropractor from Capitola, California, who was kind enough to spend time away from his popular practice to approve the exercises in the figure chapter. Also, to Mary Anne Benton, whose "Body Class" operates out of the Sports, Training and Rehabilitation Therapy Clinic in Santa Cruz, California. Mary Anne also proofed the exercises for me and is herself collaborating with an orthopedic surgeon on her own book. She also works up fitness programs for people with multiple sclerosis. Both very qualified people!
- Dolores Saluppo, my friend and a talented hairstylist at Shear Energy Hair Design in Santa Cruz, who proofed the hair chapter.
- Cindy Convisser, one of my very special students and friends, who read the manuscript from a teenager's viewpoint.
- Jean Harmon, my brilliant cousin who read my manuscript and offered not only her support and enthusiasm, but as an English

teacher in Winter Park, Florida, her professional suggestions, as well.

- Kathy Sauer and Susan Anderson, for the excellent typing jobs they did on the manuscript, despite deadlines, children, etc.
- My mother, Betsy McMillan Parks, an accomplished author herself, who not only typed the manuscript, but along with my father, Bill R. Parks, has always been there, through the good times, as well as the bad. I am very lucky to have them as my parents.
- Diane Taylor, who shared with me the beautiful wardrobe-building outline that so many of my students have successfully used.
- Kim and Sandy Brown, my friends who have always been more than willing to help out. Kim, a beautiful young woman and one of my students, helped pose for the book's illustrations.
- Kate Triplett, Shanna Laney, and Chris Malley and their wonderful families—my three courageous students who gave so much to try out for the book's cover.
- Franklin Avery; Steve Kurtz of Pacific Light Views; and Ken Kearney of Soquel and Aptos, California—all gifted photographers whose work have enhanced my own work.
- Sara Quay, an excellent hairstylist from San Francisco, California, who helped make my beautiful cover models even more beautiful by doing their hair.
- Mrs. Mary Alice Altenbach, my history teacher at East Cobb Junior High School, in Marietta, Georgia. She brought out in me the keen desire to learn and it was because of her that I went into teaching. I will never forget her.
- Julie Painchaud, my modeling teacher, and now the owner of Champagne Taste clothing boutique in San Jose, California. She helped turn me from a ''Before'' into an ''After,'' and without her belief in me, I doubt if *I* would have even had the confidence to realize *my own* potential.
- Bob Coates and Bridget McKay (now my sister-in-law!), who risked hiring an inexperienced but enthusiastic young woman for her first teaching job. I will always be grateful for their trust in me.
- All of my dear students—I have learned as much from them as they have from me.
- My husband, Tim, for enduring the endless hours away from family, so that I could turn my dreams into reality. His never-ending support helped make this book possible, and my success is his.
- Jesus Christ, my lord—my belief in Him has enabled me to get through every minute, every hour, every day.
- Finally, all the very special people I've met—who have given me their support and encouragement.

Thank you, *all* of you!

Jane Parks-McKay
Capitola, California

CONTENTS

Taking good care of our skin is the best way to enhance our natural beauty.

Body language is very important.

LET'S GET STARTED!

Hello and congratulations! You are about to begin an exciting journey of self-improvement that will change you and may even change your life. There are many benefits to self-improvement, but one of the most important is that you'll feel better about yourself, not to mention look better, and as a result you will *be* better!

We'll be working very closely together while you're reading this book. So you'll feel that I'm less of a stranger, let me tell you a little bit about myself and my background, especially as it relates to our journey together.

First of all, I know what you and many other teenagers may be going through because I've been there. I know what it feels like to be plain looking and shy. Perhaps you want to be popular and attractive? I know I did. In fact, I recall so clearly the many hours I spent pretending that I was an entirely different person: well-liked, confident, attractive. The only problem with fantasies is that you always have to come back to reality—in my case, that ugly person staring back at me in the mirror.

I think one picture is worth a thousand words, so here's what I looked like when I was a teenager, before I changed myself:

And here's what I looked like after:

How did it happen? It didn't take place overnight, believe me! I changed over a period of time. As a matter of fact, I'm still changing, and I imagine I always will be, because self-improvement is an everyday thing that never quite comes to an end. Just when I think I've become the best I can be I discover new ways to become even better. You will, too.

Here's how it all happened for me.

When I was in my early teens, my mother enrolled me in a short-term grooming course. Even though I really wanted to take the course, I was petrified. I was so scared, in fact, that after I had to introduce myself at the first class meeting, I dropped out and never went back! Even though I had many dreams, taking that first step toward making any of them come true was very difficult for me. Talking and dreaming about something is so much easier than *doing* it!

Anyway, I continued to read everything I could about beauty and self-improvement. It was really becoming an obsession with me. But that wasn't enough.

When I was fifteen, I finally worked up enough courage to try another grooming course, and I thoroughly enjoyed it. I didn't change a great deal on the outside at this point, but an important change began to happen inside me. My attitude changed. I started feeling okay about myself for the very first time. I realized I'd been letting others put me down all my life and decided to put a stop to it right away.

I also realized that before I could do anything lasting about the outside, I had to get the inside together. Gradually, a "new" me started emerging. My shyness was being replaced by an outgoing personality.

I was finally ready to change the outside.

At seventeen, about the time my "before" picture was taken, I took another, longer grooming course. This is when

I *really* changed visibly, plus even more inside. The me I had hidden for so many years was finally coming out—I was truly feeling better about myself and the world I lived in than I ever had before. I started dating, modeling professionally, and, basically, experiencing life to its fullest.

Since then I've modeled part-time and, in 1974, I opened my own image consulting business. I teach grooming, modeling, and am an image consultant for teens and adults. I've also written a beauty column for newspapers.

One of my goals was to write a book for teenagers. Why? Because, truthfully, if I can prevent you from making some of the mistakes I've made, I will feel that I've contributed something. And that's a good feeling. Plus, in my work with teenagers, I have found that some of the beauty advice you get is inaccurate, and a book like *The Make-Over* will help straighten out many misconceptions, as well as save you from wasting your time and money on needless preparations. It can also provide a good foundation for the rest of your life. I just wish straightforward advice such as this had been available when *I* was a teenager!

Working with teenagers has taught me exactly what you want to know and what you don't want to know. I've arranged the chapters as a step-by-step program, beginning with basics like your personality and ending with such finishing touches as hand care and manicure. At the end of each chapter I've included some questions I was most frequently asked in my beauty column. And since you'll be doing some exercises and various projects—which will all be fun!—you may want to keep the notes you take in a loose-leaf binder. Call it your Make-Over Notebook—I'm sure you'll want to refer back to it from time to time, and it will be easier if you keep it all together in one place.

5

What are you going to get out of this book? As much as you put into it. Self-improvement is lots of hard, consistent work; and it's not giving up, even when you feel like it. It's also just that: *self-* improvement. I can't do the work for you. Only *you* can.

You'll learn so many things; some of them you knew before but most are going to be new to you. My suggestions are basic, common-sense advice, not based on always-changing fads. Be sure to read each chapter slowly, taking the time to do every step thoroughly before going onto the next. The book is general in some areas, as most books of this kind have to be. Some situations may not apply to your personal needs. But most will. Plus, as you change, so will your needs. Keep *The Make-Over* handy, so you'll be able to refer to it frequently.

Read, study, practice, enjoy. Keep on growing, changing, and improving. But most important, dare to be the best "you" possible—you deserve it!

YOUR INNER BEAUTY

As you read through this chapter, you may wonder if you have the right book. Very often, when we think of a beauty book, we think of outside beauty, not inner beauty, which is what this chapter's all about.

As I said earlier, I really believe that before you can ever begin to work on the outside, you've got to get the inside together. Otherwise, the results aren't lasting. Don't worry—we'll get to the outside beauty aspects soon! Before we do, however, let's work on your inner beauty first.

YOU <u>ARE</u> BEAUTIFUL!

That's right, you *are* beautiful. In fact, you're probably one of the most beautiful people in the world today! Chances are you don't feel that way or even believe it, do you?

Since there are so many definitions of the word beautiful, and each one has such a bearing on the way you feel about yourself, let's start by defining what it means to you personally. What do you think the word beautiful really means? Does it speak only of the exterior, or does it go deeper, into the "inside you"?

My own definition has more to do with inner beauty. When you have that, you are confident and you look beautiful. Besides, if you don't like yourself, it's hard for anyone else to, either. Nor will you have that desire to be the best you can be, reaching to your fullest potential, without a positive attitude about yourself. Decorations, such as a new hair or makeup style, might give you a temporary lift, but they just don't do a permanent job, do they?

So then, the first step toward realizing just how beautiful you really are is to admit you *can* be beautiful. With all your fantastic characteristics, you're not stuck with the negatives nature gave you. True, certain hereditary traits may make it harder for you, but with a good, positive attitude about yourself, and the promise that you'll give it your very best, you'll be on your way to as far as you want to go!

With that in mind, relax, take a deep breath, and let's get started by finding out what you've got to work with. Once you come to terms with this, you can better accept who you are and make changes where needed.

To help you define who you are, I'm going to have you do a few self-examination exercises. They will take some serious thinking to complete, but the effort will be worth it: You'll start to see patterns emerge about yourself, and you'll also see areas you can experiment with, resulting in an even better "you"!

8

WHO AM I?
Determining Your Image

Too many people start make-over programs by copying some-one else's style, only to learn it's just not for them. They find themselves going from one image to another. Not only do they end up frustrated, but they usually lose friends along the way, as the impression they give is a false one (and that kind of a person is not very much fun to be with).

The secret is to get to know yourself first, using impressions of people you admire as guidelines *only,* then create your very own image from there. *That's* individuality.

Here's a quick test that will help you start to know yourself better. On a sheet of paper write ME at the top, then ask yourself the following questions, thinking about each one carefully before writing down your answers. There are no right or wrong answers—just *your* answers. Keep them in mind for now. They're just for "soul-searching" purposes at this point.

1. Of all the people I know, what person (female or male) do I admire the most?
2. Why did I choose this person?
3. Am I very similar to this person now?
4. If not, could I be, realistically speaking?
5. How might I specifically go about doing so?

Twenty Things You Love to Do

One way to get to know yourself better is to observe what you enjoy doing. The activities you get involved in can tell you a lot about yourself, and this exercise is a fun way of finding out just that.

9

The first step is to get a piece of paper and make a list of twenty things you love to do. They can be big things or small ones. You might think in terms of the seasons of the year or things you like to do all year round. Next, on the left-hand side of your paper, code your list in the following manner:

1. Put a dollar sign beside any item that costs more than five dollars each time it's done.

2. Place the letter *A* beside those items you prefer to do alone; the letter *P* next to those activities you prefer to do with other people; and the letters *AP* next to activities that you enjoy doing either alone or with other people.

3. Put the letters *PL* beside those items that require advanced planning.

4. The letter *N* goes next to those activities that would not have been on your list a year ago.

5. The numbers one through five are placed beside the five most important items. The best-loved activity should be numbered one, the second best two, and so on.

6. Next to each activity indicate the last time you did it.

7. Mark with an *S* any item that can only be done in one particular season of the year.

8. Put an *I* next to any item that involves intimacy (getting close, mentally or physically).

9. Place the letter *U* next to any item you have listed that you think other people would judge as unusual.

10. Put the letter *C* next to activities that you think other people might judge as very normal.

11. Use the code letters *MT* for things that you think you will want to devote more time to in the future.

12. Choose three items that you want to become better at doing. Put the letter *B* next to each one.

Like the other exercise, there aren't any right or wrong answers, just *your* answers. Take a look at your list to see if you notice a pattern about yourself. For example, in your coding, did you find that you tend to spend money on the activities you do, as opposed to the many free things available to you? Do you prefer to spend time alone, instead of with others? Does that tell you anything about yourself? (For instance, regarding future career plans, you may want to get a job that allows you to work alone instead of with a lot of people.) Also, did you find that you prefer activities that are arranged last minute or in advance? All of your coded answers will tell you something about yourself, some of which you probably didn't even realize.

Two Ideal Days

This exercise makes the point that we ought to be clear about what we want out of life. By describing two perfect days, you'll learn even more about what you really enjoy doing, which has a great bearing on how you want your life to proceed—now and for the future. Such brainstorming, as you're going to be doing, can better define what *you* want out of life, instead of what everyone else thinks you should be doing. It's certainly important to listen to others' opinions; but in the end, the final decisions are yours.

Project yourself into the future, any time from tomorrow to several years from now. Imagine two days that would, for you, be absolutely perfect. You can fantasize about whatever you want. The only limit is the time—forty-eight hours. Include where you'd be, what you'd be doing, who else might be there, and so on. Go into as much detail as you can—smells, sounds, the weather, etc. Have fun!

After you've finished, come back to reality: Do some of the

things you want to do have any relationship to how you're spending your time now or how you're planning to for the future? For example, I can recall one woman I know who, after many years of preparing for a career in business, ended up quitting because all along she wanted to be a housewife and a flamenco dancer! It seems simple, but life can get so complex sometimes that we seem to become overly concerned with expectations and not with how *we* feel about things.

Baker's Dozen

Since you probably have only a limited amount of time and money at your disposal, it's important to "prioritize"—to learn what is most important to you, what you want and value the most. For example, if I gave you a choice between chocolate or vanilla ice cream, which one would you choose? Chocolate—then you probably value chocolate more than vanilla. Vanilla? The other way around. That's what prioritizing is. By learning that, you can go about making choices, which have a bearing on everything you do, including improving yourself.

This exercise will help give you some experience in making decisions—an important skill you'll need to know the rest of your life. Make a list of thirteen things (a baker's dozen) that you use around your home that make use of electricity.

Next, draw a line through the three things you could give up most easily. For example, if there were a big energy shortage and everyone was asked to cut down on electricity usage, which three could you give up first? These are the three you'd cross out.

On the other hand, which three do you find the most pre-

12

cious? Draw circles around them. These would be the last ones you'd want to give up.

Do your answers tell you something about your priorities —the things you value the most and the least? Or, did you find that deciding among your various items was difficult? It's easy to want everything, but, unfortunately, in life, we can't have everything—that's where prioritizing comes in; it helps you decide what's most important to you and what's not.

The Pie of Life

In its simplest form, this exercise asks you to take stock of your life—to see how you actually spend your time, now as well as how you'd *like* to spend it.

Draw a large circle on a sheet of paper. Thinking of that circle as representing twenty-four hours, draw "slices" of how you spend a typical day. In other words, each slice will represent some activity (sleep, school, work, friends, homework, being alone, household chores, family, miscellaneous, etc.).

Your estimates don't have to be exact, but try to be as accurate as possible. Together the slices should add up to a complete circle of twenty-four hours. Your pie may look something like this:

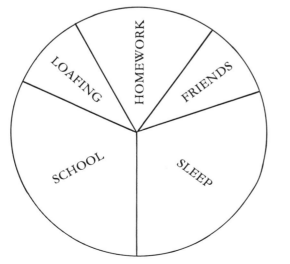

13

Now that you know how you currently spend a typical day, think of how you *should* spend it—how you can make better use of your time. Then draw another large circle and make an ideal time-pie, consisting of slices that represent activities scheduled more effectively.

Here's an example:

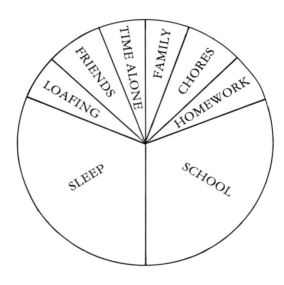

It is so easy to waste time, isn't it? While our days should include "nothing time" for having fun, if we are to accomplish what we want out of life, we need to plan our time effectively. Too, finding out how you like to spend, and not spend, your time will tell you quite a bit about yourself—your goals, your interests, your priorities. For example, if in your first pie (the one illustrating how you spend your time now), you found that you spent too much time with friends and not enough on your homework or with your family, how does that relate to your grades or your relationship with your family?

Who Comes to Your Home?

Our choice of friendships can also tell us something about our values. And values, as you know, have a lot to say about how we live our lives.

To find out even more about your values, draw a line down the middle of a piece of paper. On the left-hand side list the names of all the people you've invited to your home over the last three months. On the right side of the paper, list the names of all the people who've invited *you* to their home during the past three months.

Code both columns in the following way:

1. Put the letter *F* next to the person's name if the person was a friend, *R* for a relative, *0* for other.
2. Mark with an *M* the people whose manners bother you.
3. Star the names of those people who you're really happy to see when they come over, and on the right side, those people who you think are happy to see *you* when you come over.
4. Put an *X* if it wouldn't matter much if the person ever came back again or if the person didn't invite you to his or her home again.
5. Use *S* or *D* to indicate whether their religion is the same *(S)* or different *(D)* from yours.
6. Use *SR* or *DR* to indicate whether the person is the same race *(SR),* or a different race *(DR)* from yours.

Take a good look at your answers to see if some type of pattern emerges about yourself. What do your answers tell you about your choice in friendships? Are you spending time with people you enjoy or are you spending time with people you don't really care for? If so, why? For popularity's sake? What else? I know one girl who snubbed a perfectly nice classmate because she wasn't popular and, instead, chose to spend time with only the popular girls at school, who, in this case, were pretty snobby. Do you do that? Or have you in the past?

Who Are You Now?

As of now, you have just completed the hardest part of all this —taking a close look at yourself as you are now. This is the foundation for any type of a self-improvement program, especially this one.

So, let's take a few minutes to tie your answers all together. In the first exercise, I asked you to take a look at your self-image—how you really feel about yourself. I also asked you to compare yourself with people you admire. What did you find out? Do you like who you are now? Is that person you admire someone whose traits you can "borrow" for yourself?

When you did the Baker's Dozen exercise, was it hard for you to make some decisions about which items you'd keep and which ones you'd do away with? In other words, was it hard to prioritize? And did it get harder as you were asked to narrow down your list even more? What did you learn about yourself in this exercise?

Regarding the other exercises, you'll notice they had something to do with your time—how you spend it, what you like to do, etc. Did you find that you're spending your time the way you like to, for the most part? Are you using your time as effectively as possible? Could improvements be made? In the future, will you plan to keep these things in mind? Or, will you, like many people, get so carried away with all the things you have to do that you forget what *you* want out of life?

16

I know these are a lot of questions to consider, but they are important. If some of these questions were hard for you to answer, that's all right. Maybe you're not ready for them now, so you may want to go back to them later. If that's your case, just tuck the answers you were able to come up with in the back of your mind for now. They'll, no doubt, resurface later.

BECOMING WHO YOU WANT TO BE

As you can imagine, knowing yourself is only one part of it all. Since you are probably not altogether satisfied with certain aspects of yourself, the most important step now is to *do* something about it.

You guessed it—we're going to do a few more exercises. This time, however, your goal is to *act* upon your feelings instead of just think about them.

You may feel that you can't possibly change. Perhaps you've tried to do something about your weight, for instance, and nothing seemed to help. So, you sat back and said, "Well, I tried my best—nothing works!" That's certainly understandable, but such an attitude isn't going to do you any good. Besides, nothing ever happens overnight, even though it appears that way sometimes, so you must keep at it.

Perhaps I sound overly positive, but I really do believe there's a solution to every problem. Sometimes it's not the one you want, but it's usually the best solution for *that particular situation.* My philosophy is based upon trying your best, exploring *all* alternatives—"brainstorming," in other words. Persistence can pay off; I know, I've seen it happen in my life.

To get you started on solving your problems, try doing the following exercise.

Problem Solving

When others ask us about ourselves, too many times our answer sounds like a carbon-copied computer printout: "My name is Mary, I'm sixteen, I go to Jefferson High School, and I like sports." Right? A common mistake is to take ourselves for granted. And when we take ourselves for granted, unfortunately, others tend to take us for granted, too.

Important

So, on a sheet of paper, write down the question "Who Am I?" and think specifically about *who* you feel you really are at this point in your life. Jot down your thoughts as they come to mind.

Since this may be new to you, let me help you out by giving an example:

"I'm Mary, I'm sixteen, I'm a student at Jefferson High, and I like sports. I'm also confusing sometimes to others, as well as to myself. I'm not really sure what I want to do for a living yet. I'm happy most of the time, except that I'm overweight. I can't stand snobby people, and boys don't seem to like me much."

After you've racked your brain and exhausted the subject, get out another sheet of paper and draw a line down the middle. On the top left-hand side of the paper, write ME in capital letters and on the top right-hand side, write WHY in caps. Under the ME heading, list everything from the other piece of paper that you consider negative.

Think about each description you put about yourself, and analyze *why* you feel you're that way. Then note your reasons on the right-hand side. Let me get you started by giving you another example.

ME	WHY
Confusing sometimes to others, as well as to myself	Probably because I don't even know what I want myself, especially in the area of a career. I think I'm inconsistent, and may be confusing because of this.
I'm overweight	I like to eat more than starve. Plus, I *hate* exercising!
Boys don't seem to like me much	I don't think I have enough confidence—I'm too shy. I think it's probably because I don't feel I'm very attractive.

Now, get out another sheet of paper, draw a line down the center, and on the top left-hand side, write NEGATIVE POINTS in caps. On the top right-hand side, write HOW also in capital letters.

Referring to the negative personal characteristics you listed in the earlier part of this exercise, write the first one under the left-hand column. Having already analyzed *why* you have that particular trait, you're well on your way to possibly doing away with it.

Think about ways to eliminate that negative characteristic in the future. Write *all* the ideas that come to mind under the right-hand column. Then go through the list choosing the most realistic and workable among them and eventually crossing out the unrealistic. Do this for each of the negatives on your list. Again, I'll start you out with an example.

NEGATIVE POINTS	HOW
Confusing sometimes to others, as well as to myself	Since I'm more confused in the area of jobs, I'll spend my time and energy working on that. I'll read books and articles on different types of careers, work with my school counselor, as well as with the career center at school. I realize it'll take a while, so my best bet is to start now, before I have to make any college choices.
I'm overweight	Even though I hate dieting and exercising, I realize, deep down, I really have no choice if I want to lose weight. ~~I can join a spa, or~~ I can take an exercise class, since I probably lack some motivation of my own. With this, I can combine my regular sports activities, like bicycling, tennis, or swimming to make it more fun.
Boys don't seem to like me much	Since I feel I'm not very attractive, and this probably prevents me from becoming as confident as I'd like to be, reading this book and various beauty magazines will help me to learn how to be more attractive. A course in grooming might help, too. I'll also check into that.

20

In looking over the How column, you'll notice that for the first and third negative characteristics, "Confusing sometimes to others, as well as to myself," and "Boys don't seem to like me much" some good, honest solutions were suggested that went to the root of the problem, not around it. The second negative characteristic, "I'm overweight," had three alternative solutions. "Join a spa" was crossed out because it was unrealistic, as most spas require you to be at least eighteen years old. (But check your local ones—some are lowering the age limit, especially the aerobic dance spas.) The remaining two solutions were the most realistic and practical, in this particular case.

This should get you started turning some of those negatives into positives; but remember, once again, that no changes you attempt to make happen overnight. It takes time, patience, and more than anything else, believing that you *can* change. So, give it a good try—you'll be pleased with the results, I can assure you!

Etiquette—Better Known As Good Manners

After you start getting yourself together, you will find that your relationship with others is going to be very important. "No man is an island," a famous poet once wrote, and it's still true—we all need other people to help us reach our goals. Consequently, good manners are going to be essential.

By good manners I don't mean spending all day before going to an important dinner party wondering how to set down your napkin. I mean good manners that tell other people you care about them. When you act that way toward others, they usually respond by caring about you.

Of course, we all have different values and might carry

good manners to different lengths, but here are some basics to keep in mind.

- Try to always be on time. If you're the late type, learn not to be. Remember, you weren't born that way. You *learned* the bad habit of being late. There are quite a few good books and courses on time management. Use them.

    If you are going to be late, call the people who are expecting you. People aren't mind readers, and while they may suspect you're running late when you don't show up on time, they don't know for sure. After all, they may be worrying you've been in an accident.
- When someone does something nice for you, don't be afraid to thank them. Thank you's can be given in many ways, from verbally to thank-you notes. Many people complain that no one does anything nice for them. Maybe it's because others got tired of doing nice things for them without any thanks.
- When you promise something to someone, stick to it. You might have changed *your* mind, but how do you know *they* know that? If you're continually failing to come through with what you promised, maybe you need to improve your time management.
- Read a contemporary etiquette book. There are several good ones out that can bring you up to date on what's expected today.
- A good rule of thumb is, "If in doubt, don't." In other words, if you're not sure whether you should ask someone something, don't. At least not until you know that person better.
- Be truthful, but not blatant about it. There are lots of ways to say the same thing—the secret is to be honest but

gentle. However, don't be so gentle you forget the honesty.

- "I'm sorry" are two words many people have a hard time saying. If you blow it, admit it. Ignoring it will usually make things worse.

- When you speak, pay close attention to the way you're talking. Are you monopolizing the conversation? Do you sound too pushy? If you're rushed and are coming off too dictatorial, take a few deep breaths and calm down before speaking.

SINCE YOU ASKED . . .

Lately, I've been hanging around with some people at school whom my parents don't approve of. I'm not sure if I really like them myself all that much, but if I don't hang out with them and do what they do, they give me a hard time. What should I do?

I went through this when I was a teenager, and I think everyone does; so if it makes you feel any better, you're not alone! When I was your age, my peers were heavily involved with drugs, smoking, drinking, cutting school, etc.—the rebellious years of the sixties. Even though it appeared I was the only one, I never agreed with what my classmates were doing. I decided that I would stick with my values and not join them. Oh, I got teased unmercifully, cut down—there were some tough times. But in the end, some of the same people who put me down eventually told me how much they respected and admired me. What should *you* do? Stick with what *you* believe in. Remember, any time you say no to people, it's just human nature that they will try to talk you out of it. But you could be the winner in the end. Good luck!

Sometimes, I feel like I'm the shyest, most unconfident, and clumsiest person in the world. It just seems like all the other girls at school really

23

have it together. Am I the only one who feels this way—is there something wrong with me?

No, not at all—you're feeling just what everyone else feels, and, if you were to look a little closer at these other girls at school and get to know them, you'd be surprised to find that they feel the same way! Make friends with some of the girls you admire. You might end up learning things from each other!

You talk about confidence and feeling good about yourself. I know this may sound stupid, but how do you feel confident, how do you get over shyness? I feel so uncomfortable with people, and I'd like to change; but I don't know how.

Good question, and don't feel bad about asking it. What I did to get over my extreme shyness when I was a teenager was to come to terms with my own self-worth. I had let other people put me down so badly for so many years that I was beginning to feel worthless myself. Then, one day when I hit bottom, I looked at myself and found that even though I did need a lot of improvement, I was still a worthwhile person—a "diamond in the rough," as the old saying goes. Instead of just sitting around wishing I weren't shy, I did something about it: I took courses, read, asked questions, but mainly, I forced myself to do things that I wouldn't normally do—go to school dances, talk with people at school I didn't normally talk with. At first, it was really hard; but the more I did it, the easier I found it to be. In fact, even now, when I find myself feeling a bit shy about something (yes, I'm still basically shy, believe it or not!), I force myself to do it, and it always works. Remember, it's the *starting* that's the hardest. Once you get going, it's a piece of cake!

24

Every time I see some girl who's so pretty, I get depressed. I've tried to make myself as pretty as possible—I've made use of my positive points, as you suggest—but I still get depressed sometimes. What do I do? I feel stuck with what I have.

First of all, change your attitude—quit comparing yourself to others so much. It's all right to do that every now and then, but start spending the energy looking into yourself more. You say that you've made use of your positive points. Are there any other areas you can improve upon to realize your full potential? Have you tried everything? Probably not. The one thing you've got to remember is that *everyone* is beautiful, and that includes you. Don't try to be better than others—try to be better than *you've* been. It works!

Now that you've worked on the most important part of yourself—your inner beauty—it's time to work on your outer beauty.

3

DRESSING
FOR
YOUR
STYLE

Handwritten notes in left margin:

- Know who I'm & creatively express myself using clothes & fashion.
- Buy a few good quality clothes.
  Because I may change over time & also, the trend keeps changing.
  I may need to adjust my wardrobe on an annual basis.
  Hence, a good way to save money is to buy a few good quality clothing to express my Real self.
- p.40 ~46
1. Know what looks good on me
2. Use what I have to express my true self & my style.
   To do this effective as well as shop effectively, I need to organize my wardrobe & do an inventory
3. From the inventory, I find out what I need to buy.

   My intention is consistent with hers & others'.

HE BIGGEST MISTAKE PEOPLE make with their clothing is that they dress only according to what is in style. While many new fashions are very attractive, not all of them are meant for everyone. Therefore, it's important to determine which styles are for *you.*

In putting together a wardrobe, your goal should be to express your own style, your individuality, without going too far off the deep end. You'll feel more comfortable with your look. Plus, your clothing will express who you are to others —the *real* key to dressing.

WHAT <u>IS</u> YOUR STYLE?

Before we go into developing your own style, let's take a few minutes to see how much style you have now.

Get out a sheet of paper and recall how you projected yourself last year at this time—the clothing you wore, your

26

makeup, your hairstyle, etc. Jot down a description on the paper. Then write down the reasons for anything you've changed or didn't change. Your answers will tell you quite a bit about yourself, and how much you've changed!

Next, ask yourself who you dress for—yourself or others—and why. Like the exercises in the previous chapter, there aren't any right or wrong answers to these questions, so be honest with yourself.

for myself
express myself using clothing & fashion
Attract the RIGHT people.

Now, jot down your answers to these questions:

What is your approach to dressing? In other words, from the time you get up in the morning, to the time you leave the house, what goes on in your mind regarding what to wear? The people you're going to see? Where you're going? To give you an example, here's my approach: I always look out the window to see what the weather is like. Then, I choose what I'm going to wear based on the weather, my mood, and my plans for the day. What's your approach?

My approach now is similar to hers.

Also, think about whether or not you "package" yourself. To give you an example, let's use a gift. You can either throw the gift into a paper bag, then give it to someone as a present; or you can package it: decorate it with wrapping paper, bows, a card on the top, etc. Dressing is done very much the same way. Do you put yourself together carefully, or do you throw yourself together? If your answer is throw yourself together, ask yourself why.

I now put myself together carefully.
why?
I love myself.
I'm worthy & valuable.

Next, what's your favorite outfit, right now? Jot down your answer, and ask yourself why it came to mind. Does the style make you feel great, or is it just plain comfortable? At the same time, think about your least favorite outfit. Jot the answer down, and the reasons why you don't like it. Your answers will give you good information for future clothing purchases, too.

27

Do an inventory

Now, open up your closet doors and take a good look at what you have. Does most of your wardrobe consist of clothing you like, at least a little bit, or is most of it things you could take or leave? Make a note of your findings.

In looking through your closet, see if your clothing reflects the "real you" (that is, who you *really* are) or the "ideal you" (who you'd like to be but maybe aren't). For example, take someone who's a very feminine type yet wears sporty clothing, just because it's in style at the moment. She'd be dressing more for the ideal her, not the real her, and should be wearing clothing more in line with her personality—at least most of the time. It's all right to dress according to fashion; but if that works against your personality, you'll probably feel uncomfortable and unnatural.

color

Also, what are your favorite colors? And what are your least favorite colors? I've found that many people tend to like some of the colors that are best for them, which is a pleasant surprise!

Good exercise

One last way of finding and developing your own style is to use an "image journal." You'll find it comes in handy when you're thinking about improving or changing your style. Very simply, it's put together this way: Start collecting pictures of looks you like and looks you don't like, and store them in a folder. When you feel you've collected enough pictures, go through them to see if you notice any pattern about your tastes and personality. I recently put together an image journal myself and found that my tastes had changed from the dressy look I had been wearing for several years to a more casual, simple look.

Now, take a look at all of your answers. As in the last chapter, did you notice any pattern about yourself, however small? Gone are the days of simply putting something on

28

because it's in fashion. Again, the way you dress can tell the world quite a bit about yourself, and if you don't know who you are, you can't really project that to others.

For example, look at your answer to the question about how you projected yourself last year at this time. Have you changed? A lot? A little? Do you like your look now? Why, or why not? Does your present way of dressing, making up, etc. reflect the changes that are going on inside you, or are they still based on what you think others want you to look like?

Who do you dress for—yourself or others? Of course, we all dress for different people, including ourselves, at various times. But *mostly,* who do you dress for? If you found that you dress for others, then doesn't that tell you that you might be caring a bit too much about others' opinions and not enough about your own? What makes *you* comfortable?

Did you find that you package yourself, or do you stop short of it? Is that what makes you feel the best? Or, deep inside, are you yearning to look more together, more packaged? If so, what's stopping you? What do *you* want to do? If time is stopping you, then you may want to look over how you manage your time. If you leave just a few minutes to get ready in the morning, then you may want to change your schedule a bit, allowing more time to work on your appearance.

How about your approach to dressing? What did you find out? Are you putting yourself together in accordance with your plans for the day? Are you dressing appropriately?

What else do your answers tell you? How about your favorite and least favorite outfits? Years ago, when I was changing my image, I found that my closet was full of blouses that had to be tucked inside tight pants and skirts—the look at the time. I realized that since I hadn't been wearing much of what was in my closet, I really disliked anything that was uncomfortable feeling—things that were too tight and binding. I preferred things that were more flowing and looser-fitting. So I adjusted my wardrobe accordingly. What do your findings tell you?

Finally, what did your Image Journal tell you about yourself? As I mentioned, when I did my last one, I found that I was attracted to more of a casual look. This was something that I certainly suspected, but my Image Journal helped me better define what my likes, as well as my dislikes, were.

Remember, as you change, so will your values. Therefore, periodically, you'll probably want to go back and answer again the questions you just went through.

WHAT TO WEAR: ANALYZING YOUR FIGURE

As I mentioned earlier, wearing what's new in fashion would be great if you looked like everyone else. However, all you have to do is look around to find that all of us have entirely different features: some good, some not so good! Before we go into the details of what's best for you, let's start by analyzing your figure. Quite a bit of what you should be wearing depends upon your figure.

Close your eyes and think about your body—its positive as well as negative points. Come on—now's *not* the time to be too complimentary about yourself! Concentrate your mind's attention on your bustline. Is it too small, too large? How about your waistline? Spreading fast? Your hips—too large or too small? What about your arms and legs? Are they a little too thick or thin?

There now, wasn't that much easier and less painful than

30

you thought it would be? Remember what you noticed, because you'll find it useful for the next section.

Optical-Illusion Dressing

Now that you have a better idea of what you have to work with, the goal with your clothing is to accentuate the positive and camouflage or cover up the negative. If you think this can't be done, then lucky you—you're in for a nice surprise!

By creating an optical illusion, you can practically reshape any part of your body just by selecting the right garments. We all know that most of us have not been given a perfect figure. But there are some things that can be done to give the appearance of smallness or largeness, as well as slimness or width. It's all done by optical illusion: bringing others' attention to your positive points rather than advertising your negative ones.

To start with, *color* plays an important role in creating optical illusions. Dark colors decrease size, and light colors increase size. If you have a small bustline, your best bet is to concentrate on lighter, brighter colors around that area; for a spreading waistline, darker colors.

To visualize this effect better, imagine yourself in a small room decorated with dark colors and brown shutters. That room would probably give you a cramped feeling. However, if that same room were decorated with lighter colors, it would give you a roomier feeling, wouldn't it?

Getting back to fashion, color can be applied to accessories, as well. Light-colored shoes will make a narrow foot appear wider. With the reappearance of the belt over the last few years, if you have a larger-than-desired waistline and feel you really must wear a belt, try to stick with a darker, thinner one,

31

or preferably, one whose color blends in with your outfit.

Knowing which colors are best for you is important, too, not only for the look you project but for the way you feel. To get a general idea of which colors are right for you, drape a large, solid-colored piece of beige fabric next to your face (with no make-up) and across your shoulders; then, replace it with a solid white piece of fabric. Determine which color looks better on you, looking at the overall impression you receive—not just how your skin, eyes, or hair may look with the color. For example, instead of comparing only your eye color with the swatch, you'll want to sit a couple of feet away from a large mirror and see how each swatch looks on you *as a whole.* It's easy to mistake one color as being good for you if you just compare it with one of your features. But since others look at *all* of us, not just one part, that's what you're going to have to look at, too.

If you look best in the beige color, you probably have a warm-colored complexion and would look best in the warm version of most colors. If you look best in the white color, your complexion is probably a cool-toned one, so select colors that are cooler versions. To determine whether a color is warm or cool, ask yourself what general feeling you get when you look at it. If it looks warm, glowing (not bright), and earthy, it's probably warm; if it looks cool, sedate, almost foresty in feeling, it's probably cool.

Of course, to fully understand warm versus cool colors, you have to see them visually; even then, it takes a while to grasp. So don't get too worried about this now.

An example will help you understand this better. Take green, for instance. There are both warm and cool versions of this color. If you look at a moss green, you'll probably notice it's a bit yellowy looking, isn't it? Does it give you a

32

sunny, warm feeling? If so, it's probably a warm color. On the other hand, consider a blue-green. It's usually more toward the cool side. Why? Because it probably evokes a colder feeling inside you—as if you're standing deep inside a chilly rain forest.

To give yourself some practice with colors, test yourself with your own clothing. Even though some items may be difficult to identify as warm or cool, there are bound to be others that are easy to classify. And, for now, that's fine.

However, if you're still not sure what colors are generally best for you, I'd suggest reading some of the excellent color books out on the market for guidance. Then, if you want, schedule an appointment with a good color consultant. He or she will be able to select some of the exact colors most flattering to you.

There are many people doing colors now, and of course, some are better than others. So, do your homework and ask a lot of questions before committing your time and money to anyone. Here's what to ask. Find out about their training— specifically, how much they've had. Some consultants don't have the proper background about color. Instead, many today are trained to drape you with many, many colors, according to some type of generic formula, without really understanding how color theory works. Result: You'll end up getting a color palette identical to many other people's, not just for *you*. Instead, what you're looking for is someone who has studied color theory in depth (similar to the knowledge an art background can bring) and who can explain how and why each color relates to *your* skin, hair, eyes, etc. You will find the services of a qualified color consultant to be very effective, and what you learn will allow you to make more educated choices in the future.

Any Specialist
1. My needs
2. Does he know how to use his expertise to satisfy my needs.

Also, find out how much experience they've had. Remember, though, that if they're new it doesn't mean they don't know what they're doing. The key here is potential. Are they good at communicating? Do they seem reliable? How do they present themselves? If possible, ask to attend one of the free lectures they probably give. That will help answer a lot of questions.

Also, if necessary, have them supply references to you. Have they done colors for anyone you know? Call the Better Business Bureau or your local chamber of commerce. Check to see if they have a business license from city hall. Most cities require it. Above all, use your intuition. Do you feel comfortable with them?

This may seem like a lot to go through, but the effort may save you a lot of money, not to mention the embarrassment of wearing colors completely wrong for you!

A second concept in optical illusion dressing is *line.* Take a look at the drawing to the left. You'll notice there are two lines—one vertical (up and down) and one horizontal (left to right). Which line looks longer? The vertical line, right? Yet, both lines are identical in length!

You can apply line to your clothing by using this concept. To look slimmer, wear clothing that has vertical lines to it, instead of a horizontal look, which tends to widen. Examples of vertical lines are vertical stripes and buttons; belts are horizontal lines. In the case of skirts, an A-line skirt will slim a hipline, and a dirndl skirt will add to it. The concept of line can also be applied to necklines. Square necklines will make a person appear larger-busted; so will round necklines. However, deep V-necklines will usually make the bustline appear flatter. Necklines can also emphasize or disguise certain face shapes. For instance, if you have a square-shaped face, you'll

34

want to stay away from square necklines. Otherwise, you're only bringing out the squareness in your jaw. Instead, wear necklines that are more rounded. If your face is long and narrow, you'll want to wear rounded or square necklines that minimize length. As you can imagine, a V-neckline would make your face shape look longer. If your face is round, that's when a V-neckline will help, as it adds length to your face; a rounded neckline will make your face look rounder.

Hemlines are another area where this concept applies. Generally, the longer the hemline, the slimmer you'll look. Lengths above the knee tend to cut you visually in two, therefore making you appear shorter and wider; longer hemlines will normally make you appear slimmer.

In the area of shoes, short chunky heels will make slim legs look fatter; high, narrow heels will make legs appear slimmer.

③ In addition to color and line, *pattern* plays an important role in optical-illusion dressing. Large patterns will increase size visually. For example, you've probably seen huge women wear large floral prints. Although they probably believe they're hiding their weight, they're not; if anything, they're bringing attention to it!

Scarves worn around the neck will make that area appear larger. Ruffles and other busyness will also, as will jewelry, especially larger pieces. Garments with smaller patterns, however, will usually make you appear smaller. There is an exception: If the small patterns are spaced far apart, they'll give the appearance of a large pattern, which will make you appear larger than you are.

④ In planning their wardrobe, many people leave out *fabric texture,* the fourth concept in optical-illusion dressing.

An airy, fluffy, light-feeling fabric, such as cotton or voile, will make you appear larger; so will a heavy fabric with a nap,

35

such as corduroy. On the other hand, if you'd like to minimize certain areas, such as your hips, your best bet is to stay with fabrics that are neither fluffy nor thick, such as gabardine. Although this fabric is a bit heavy feeling, it does give a slimming appearance, and that's what you're after here.

Keep in mind, too, that thinner fabrics, such as silk, will usually emphasize any figure problem you have, whether you're too thin or heavy. In other words, if you're bony or chunky in any area, don't wear a too-revealing fabric there.

To see what I mean, go to your closet and find a few items made of different types of fabric. Close your eyes and feel the weight of each piece of fabric, feel the texture, and notice the impression each gives you. Try to mentally apply it to your figure type. Also, consider your skin when choosing texture. For example, if you have a smooth, "peaches and cream" complexion, you can get away with smoother, shinier fabrics. However, if your skin is blotchy and bumpy, a smooth, shiny fabric will only bring the blotchiness out more. Therefore, the best texture for you to use, especially closer to your face, is a rougher, looser weave with less smoothness and shininess.

It's one thing to read about optical-illusion dressing, but it's another to try and put it into practice. Whether you're using optical-illusion dressing now, or will be when shopping in the future, I'd suggest going through this six-step process. Practice doing it now and the next time you're out shopping, even if you don't intend to buy anything. Here's how it works:

First of all, when you're trying to determine whether something's right for you, analyze your figure, particularly your bustline, waistline and hipline. Decide which areas you'd like to emphasize or hide.

Steps two through five are to apply the four optical-illusion concepts discussed previously—color, line, pattern, and texture, deciding what is right or wrong for you.

Step number six is the most important one—making a decision. Based on what you've found out, determine whether the garment is something that's right for you or not. Remember, nothing's perfect, so don't seek perfection. Instead, determine whether the garment is *generally* for you or not. For example, if you found the color, line, and pattern to be good for you, then buy or keep the garment. However, if few of the concepts check out, it's time to go on to another garment and reject that one.

TURNING A BLAH BASIC INTO A GORGEOUS "WOW"

Accessorizing is a great way to look super; it also adds "mileage" to what you already have. By using jewelry, hair accessories, shoes, handbags, and belts, you can make a basic outfit, such as this one, look a variety of ways:

The secret to accessorizing is knowing what style of accessories to wear, how much to wear, and how large the pieces should be.

The key point to remember here is to keep it simple. No matter how many new looks there are in accessories, the best investment you can make is in simpler styles—they're always in fashion. Remember, you're trying to draw attention to *you,* not the accessory! Plus, you'll find that your accessories will go with more of your clothing and occasions, leaving you extra money to spend on other things. For example, I have a pair of plain gold earrings I wore on my wedding day *and* that I now wear to work!

This illustration shows some examples of basic accessories that will work for you beautifully. As you can see, they're all very simply designed and, by themselves, might appear boring, but when teamed with your clothing, they'll look terrific.

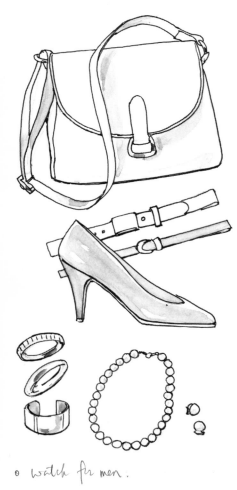

o watch for men.

Regarding color choices, try to keep the color of your accessories within the same color family. In other words, if you're wearing gold-colored jewelry, you'd want to complete the look by wearing shoes in the brown color family and carrying a handbag in a similar color as well. On the other hand, if you're prone toward silver-colored jewelry, you'd find shoes and a handbag in the black color family to go quite nicely with it. Although your accessories don't have to match each other exactly, the most important thing is that they *complement* one another. Mixing golds and silvers, blacks and browns, etc. looks tacky!

The amount of accessories you wear is something to consider, too. You don't want to look underaccessorized, but you don't want to look overaccessorized, either. The secret is *balance.* Depending upon what your personality is and where you're going, a good balance of accessories is: earrings, necklace, ring, bracelet, shoes, and handbag. However, there are exceptions: For example, if you're wearing an outfit that has a lot of detail in it (such as patterns, ruffles, etc.) and your hair is curly, you'd want to keep accessories to a minimum. Otherwise, you'd be too busy-looking, as the curly hair acts somewhat as an accessory to your look. Of course, if you don't like bracelets, don't feel that you have to wear them. There are many variables to consider in deciding on accessories, and the best guide to use is your good judgment. If in doubt, don't.

Finally, consider the size of accessories. It's common sense, but you'd be amazed how many small-boned people I've seen wearing super-large accessories, and vice-versa, just because they're the newest rage. The main thing to keep in mind is, if you're medium to large-boned, go for larger pieces; small-boned, smaller pieces. That applies to all types of accessories, including handbags.

TURNING YOUR CLOSET INTO A BEST-DRESSED ONE

Have you ever opened your closet doors and announced you didn't have a thing to wear? Then this section is especially for you.

Before you convince yourself that you need a whole new closetful of clothing, stop and take a look at what you already own. Chances are, you have the makings of a beautiful wardrobe right now. But before it can be as workable as possible, you've got to do some organizing first.

1. Start by taking *everything* out of your bureau drawers and closet. Go through each and every item (that's right— remember, to *get* something you have to *give* a bit; that's how the beautiful become beautiful!) and determine

39

whether it falls into the desirable or undesirable category. Desirables are those items you like or feel good in; undesirables are items that have been hanging in your closet almost forever or things that have bad memories and you never wear them.

Discard your undesirables by making money from them. You're not accomplishing anything by leaving them in your closet, are you? Have a garage or yard sale with friends, rent a space at a local flea market, place an ad in your local newspaper, distribute index cards on bulletin boards in laundromats.

The best method I've found is to sell them to a consignment store. In most cases, they'll sell your garments for about half the price you paid for them, and, when sold, you'll find this brings in some extra money that you can reinvest in new clothing. To find a consignment store near you, look in the *Yellow Pages* under Used Clothing.

Or, if you prefer, give them to a charity in your town. This is not only a good solution for unwanted clothes, but it benefits others, too.

2. While you're discarding your undesirables, now's the time to work with the items you kept. Repair them, sew on loose buttons, and finish undone hems. <u>Make sure your wardrobe is ready to wear. It'll save you lots of time and frustration.</u>

<u>Also, wash items you've been meaning to wash, clean your accessories, take items that need to be professionally cleaned to the dry cleaners.</u> If you're low on money and you've got lots of garments to take, take a small amount at a time, starting with your favorites.

3. Speaking about cleaning, there's nothing more timewast-

ing than clean clothes in a dusty closet. Take this opportunity to wipe down walls and shelves with a damp cloth. Vacuum (or sweep, if you have a hardwood floor) all closet floors, and dust bureau drawers. It's amazing how fast dust collects, and how fast clean clothes get soiled.

4. Last, but certainly not least, to really start seeing the rewards of all your work, categorize your wardrobe. I've seen many good methods, but the one I recommend is to group tops and blouses together, pants together, skirts together, and dresses together. You'll get more mileage out of your closet this way. Plus, you're opening up the possibility for outfit combinations you never saw before.

I'm using this system.

All of this is a lot of work but, believe me, you'll find it to be a real money and time saver in the long run.

Now comes the payoff for the organizing you've just done. To actually see for yourself how much you already have in your closet and to prevent yourself from wearing the same thing over and over again, you're going to put together a Wardrobe-Building Outline. I think you'll find it to be quite helpful. (Remember, however, that if you're going to get out of this project everything you possibly can, you've got to organize your closet first.)

The outline is easy. Take out all of your blouses and tops and match each one with your pants and skirts. Then jot down each combination on a sheet of paper, as I've done in the sample outline that follows. Use the same method with the rest of your wardrobe. Although you won't be able to mix and match your dresses as you can your separates, you may be able to use a few of them as tunics over pants. So you may want to include them anyway on your outline for reference.

Also, be sure to coordinate in your vests, sweaters, jackets, etc.—anything that varies your outfit. You'll be surprised how many looks you can get out of just one item!

To find out how many combinations you came up with, count the number of garments you worked with, the combinations from your chart, and note that at the top of your outline. Then, as you put on each combination, jot down the date you wore it. That way, when you find yourself reaching out of habit for "old faithful," you'll see that you just wore it!

To force yourself to use this system, keep the outline (and a pencil) near your closet and refer to it when deciding what to wear.

Here's what a portion of your Wardrobe-Building Outline could look like:

WARDROBE-BUILDING OUTLINE
75 garments — 150 outfits

GARMENT	COMBINATIONS
orange blouse	orange skirt—6/14
	beige pants
	white pants
black top	orange skirt—6/1
	long black skirt
	beige pants
	white pants
green blouse	bone skirt—6/16
	brown pants
	aqua skirt

It's easy, isn't it? It's incredible how many outfits you can get out of your wardrobe, and how much money and time this system will save you, isn't it? Plus, you'll look great!

SHOPPING CREATIVELY

Once you have your wardrobe together and begin using the Wardrobe-Building Outline, you'll find that you'll start making much wiser clothing purchases than in the past.

Here are some shopping tips that will insure even better investments for you. With the price of clothing these days, that's exactly what shopping is—investing!

First, always make a specific list. Too often, I see people wandering around with no definite idea in mind—a great way to buy what you really don't need. Be sure to check over your Wardrobe-Building Outline before you shop. There will be some garments that need more combinations, so use it as a guide. Don't forget to update it, particularly as you add new things and eliminate old items. If you're starting from scratch, invest in basic separates—they're *always* in fashion! That way, you can mix and match them for lots of different looks. Depending upon your tastes and lifestyle, some good, basic items might include two blouses, two skirts, two pairs of pants, a couple of jackets, vests and sweaters, and perhaps a basic coat —all in colors that will coordinate with each other. Remember, though, being "safe" doesn't always mean being boring. I knew someone who, in an effort to be practical, stocked her wardrobe full of varying shades of brown! Other colors *can* be used!

If you're starting from scratch on accessories, you may want to go for a pair of earrings, a necklace (in gold or silver), a neutral-colored belt (something in the brown family if you

what is the basic for men?

43

like gold-colored jewelry; the black family, if you like silver-colored jewelry), and a pair of basic shoes in brown, black, or bone. Also, you may want to get a handbag, either in the brown or black families, or bone, if you buy bone-colored shoes.

2 Second, decide ahead of time where you're going to shop. Otherwise, you'll end up wasting a lot of time running around, especially if you are going to be shopping in a large city or shopping mall with several clothing stores.

3 Next, when you enter the store, go directly to the department you're interested in. Check sale items first, then regular stock. There may be some nice things on sale, and if you can get the same thing less expensively, why not? However, don't reject something simply because of price. "Investment Dressing" is the term to remember here. For example, you may find something that's priced extremely low, but before you jump for joy, ask yourself how much usage you're going to get out of it. The price tag should only be one of many considerations when shopping.

4 Fourth, when you find something you like, remember to apply the six-step technique that we covered earlier: analyze your figure; decide whether the color, line, pattern, and texture are right for the goals you want to achieve; then make a decision about whether it's generally for you or not. At this time, also check the quality of the garment. If it's priced high and the quality is poor, you may want to consider looking around more.

5 If your selection has passed all these tests, then it's time to try the garment on. Never take clothing you wouldn't ever buy into the fitting room. It's not a good use of your time, nor is it fair to the store.

If you like it on you, check the side and back views in a

44

three-way mirror—proper fit is important. Finally, buy it only if you're sure. If you're not, you can always put it on hold if it's not a sale item. That way, you can give the item more thought without feeling pressured. Plus, the store won't charge you anything—as opposed to putting it on "layaway."

Since shopping creatively may be new to you, I'd suggest a practice shopping trip before the real thing (that means don't spend any money). It's fun, and you'll learn from the practice. Make it an enjoyable experience—treat yourself to lunch and people-watching (two of *my* favorite things).

Shopping is Fun & can be a creatively activity!

It's one thing to talk about some shopping generalities. It's another to get down to basics—like your feet. Proper-fitting shoes are essential to your outlook and to the kind of day you're going to have. Many people are notorious for buying fashionable shoes that don't fit.

Always plan to shop for shoes late in the afternoon. By then your feet will have swollen to their largest size of the day. Also, try not to buy shoes around the time of your monthly period. Many girls retain water; if you do, too, you wouldn't get a true fit.

Shoes

Have the salesperson measure both of your feet. One foot is usually a bit larger than the other. Properly fitting shoes should be at least a half-inch longer than the longest toe—this gives you "wiggling room."

Never, ever break in new shoes. If shoes don't fit when you buy them, they usually won't break in—they'll end up breaking *you* instead!

Regarding heel height, doctors usually recommend anywhere from one-half inch to one and three-quarter inches. Heels higher than that shift the body's weight forward, bringing on problems such as swayback and fatigue. A high, narrow

45

heel can also strain your knee and ankle joints and, if worn over a period of time, can shorten the calf muscles and tighten the heel cords. Remember, your feet will have to carry you through a lifetime, so treat them right from the start.

When buying socks and pantyhose, buy correct sizes here, too. If varicose veins run in your family, your best bet is to start wearing support hose now—in both socks *and* pantyhose. They're usually a bit more expensive, but they will help prevent future problems.

PUTTING IT ALL TOGETHER

So, you know what looks good on you, you've organized your wardrobe, and you know how to shop creatively. What next? How do you put it all together in your closet and bureau drawers so you can always stay on top of yourself? New habits are only as good as the organization behind them!

First of all, as I said earlier, clothing should be organized into categories: blouses together, pants together, etc. Categorize garments you store in bureau drawers, too, with the most frequently worn items on top, which will save you time.

Hang your necklaces, belts, and scarves on nails or hooks attached to your closet wall—this really keeps everything untangled. Regarding your shoes, you may want to store them in their original boxes. Not only does this method save space, but the boxes help prevent dust build-up. Label each box according to what's inside. That way, you won't have to search through each box to find the shoes you're looking for.

Handbags can also be grouped together on a shelf; and, if you don't have a bureau drawer, put all panties, hosiery, bras, and other lingerie categorized separately on an easily accessible shelf. To prevent wood from snagging the delicate fabric, tape paper towels onto the shelves' surfaces.

46

As you can see, these suggestions aren't very glamorous—there are no fancy wallpapers, shelf paper, or jewelry hangers. As much as you'd like to have all that, do you really *need* it? Wouldn't you rather spend your money on other things?

SINCE YOU ASKED . . .

Some days I just feel like being a slob in the way I look. Is it really necessary to be "on" all the time with my looks?

Absolutely not! One of the things I resent most is having to look perfect all the time, especially in *my* job. If you want to have an occasional kick-back day, that's fine, in my opinion. But I think the word to remember here is "appropriate." For example, if you're just going to be around the house or with some friends who wouldn't mind you looking that way, go ahead. But you certainly wouldn't want to show up at a special party looking like a slob, would you? If you did, and it wouldn't be appropriate, don't go. You'd be doing everyone a favor, including yourself! I really feel that our looks should be an expression of who we are inside, as well as where we are going and who we are going to be with. My guidelines are great for those days you want to look your best.

I don't really like to carry handbags, except for special occasions. Instead, I usually carry a backpack, especially to school. But I still want to look well-groomed. Is a handbag really necessary? Also, what style and colors should I look for?

If you feel more comfortable not carrying a handbag, that's fine. And I'm glad you consider your backpack a part of your outfit. You'd be surprised how many well-groomed people I've seen carrying backpacks that are ready to fall apart—it really destroys their whole image. As far as style, this consideration is certainly tied into what your needs are. For exam-

47

ple, if you tend to carry quite a bit, then you're looking for a backpack that has a large capacity. Remember, however, if you want that backpack to go with as many of your outfits as possible, you'll want to look for basic styling—nothing that has lots of snaps, labeling, etc. Regarding color, something neutral but easy to clean would be your best bet. Even though an ivory color would go with everything, it would show dirt faster, so stick with something in the brown or black color families, depending upon your own taste.

I really like pretty accessories. Is there anything wrong with having a few items in my closet that aren't so basic?

A Good Tip

No, not at all! The only reason I suggest basic styles in accessories and clothing is because today everything is so expensive; if you want to get as much mileage as possible out of each dollar you spend on your clothing, the more basic you go, the better. However, I definitely think that if you can afford it, it's always fun to have something less than practical in your closet. The main thing, though, is to *concentrate* on basic items and supplement them with other things, if you like.

I like to dress as many different ways as possible because it's fun. In reading that you prefer to see people stick with a style of their own, do you think I'm projecting confusion to others by not sticking with just one look? I think I'd get bored if I just looked one way.

You may be projecting confusion, but then again, you may not; it all depends upon how you do it. Let me emphasize that I don't think everyone should project just one look—yes, I agree that it would be boring! Instead, it's more a matter of finding various looks that fit *your* style. And, if *your* style is looking different at various times, then I doubt if you're confusing people.

48

I need new glasses. Can you give me any suggestions as to what type of frames are best for my features?

Since you haven't described your facial features, I'll give some general guidelines. If your face is round, try wearing glasses with squared frames. On the other hand, if your face is on the square side, get frames with rounded edges. If you have small features, small frames would look best on you; with large features, bigger frames. Also, the color of the frames should never be darker than your hair color—this makes you look too harsh; and the top of the frames should, ideally, follow the arch of your brow in order to get that natural look.

4

ENHANCING YOUR NATURAL BEAUTY WITH COSMETICS

EVEN IF YOU DON'T WEAR makeup often, won't it be nice to know how to use cosmetics, just in case you'd like to? The best way to get that natural look you're going for is to start with the basics—namely, regular, effective skin care. Skin is a sensitive organ and responds to the care you give it.

Many people tend to neglect their skin, thinking of their complexions as permanent fixtures they can forget about and take for granted. They cover up their less-than-attractive skins with cosmetics in the hope this will make them beautiful. Not so!

Since some of this lack of care can be blamed on the fact that many people consider skin to be a boring subject, let's begin by thinking about your skin in a more positive way.

GETTING TO KNOW YOUR "BIRTHDAY SUIT"

You've probably never really thought about your skin—it's just there. Yet it's the largest organ of your body. Although average skin measures one-tenth of an inch in thickness, if you were to take only about a square inch of skin, you'd find that within that tiny area there are about 78 nerves, 650 sweat glands, 20 blood vessels, 78 sensory heat regulators, 13 sensory cold regulators, 1,300 nerve endings to record pain, 19,500 sensory cells, 165 pressure apparatus, 100 sebaceous glands, 65 hairs, 65 muscles, and 15,500,000 cells. Amazing, isn't it?

Not only are its contents incredible, but skin performs some important functions, as well. First of all, it cools you off by perspiring when you're hot and keeps you warm when the weather is cold simply by its presence. It produces vitamin D —essential for good health—with the help of the sun. Plus, skin acts as a mirror. When you haven't been taking good care of yourself, it lets you and the rest of the world know.

Your skin is fragile and must be treated properly if it is to remain in the best possible condition. For example: Skin is elastic; it stretches over your frame like a rubber band. If you regularly pull, stretch, or bully it, it will stretch out of shape, and usually *stay* that way. *No* product will ever permanently shrink it back to the way it was. Many people believe that using upward strokes lifts the skin and prevents eventual sagging. But when you really think about it, whether you're pulling your skin upward, downward, or sideways, you're still *pulling* it. Use a gentle, circular motion instead.

It is also important to cleanse your skin on a regular basis. Cleanse your face at least twice a day, *every* day (including holidays). For oily complexions, cleanse three times a day, if possible. Even if you have a busy schedule, do it. Skipping your routine will bring on disastrous results. You're only hurting yourself, when you get right down to it.

Also, keep your routines simple. In fact, the simpler the better. For example, if you use a mask on your face, which makes your skin appear smoother and removes excess dirt, it may give your skin a better texture temporarily. However, research has indicated that frequent usage of such products may, in fact, provoke broken blood vessels, especially if the mask is a *very* tightening kind. If you use a commercially made mask, try to use one that isn't too tightening. It won't constrict the blood vessels quite as much. To find out how tight the mask is before buying it, try testing it on your hand. Wait a few minutes to see how tight it gets. If there aren't any testers available, ask the salesperson about it. Most masks today aren't as tightening as they once were, so most products on the market will probably be fine. Remember, too, that masks especially designed for an oily complexion are going to be quite a bit more tightening than those made for a dry complexion, so don't get too alarmed.

You can also make your own masks at home, but be sure to use fresh ingredients and clean containers—these precautions will decrease the chance of infection. To find out more about making and using your own cosmetics, check your local bookstore for books on the subject. Also, beauty and health magazines occasionally carry articles on this topic so keep your eye out. Use a mask only about once a week, and make sure you use the right kind for your skin type—more on just that in the next section.

Steaming the face regularly, long believed to open the

pores and flush out excess oil, is generally not effective for deep cleansing of the oil glands. Why? Basically, there are two types of openings on the skin's surface—a sweat pore and an oil pore. When hot steam or water is placed on the skin, the sweat pores react by opening up, producing more sweat. However, the oil pores react by doing the opposite—closing. So, when you're steaming your face, you're not really cleaning out your oil glands as much as you're cleaning out your sweat pores. Steaming *does* help clean out impurities that are found in perspiration, though, so I would suggest doing it for that purpose.

Also, when using any skin-care products, try to use the unscented one if you can, no matter what your skin type. Technically, most, if not all, products have some scent. If they didn't, the odor might be pretty bad! However, what you should look for is a product that doesn't have a fragrance added, *in addition.* While nice-smelling, such fragrances might irritate your skin. It's best to look for the word "unscented" on the label.

A discussion on the treatment of skin would not be complete without mentioning sun exposure. While a little sun is important to the skin, too much of it can be disastrous. Not only does prolonged sun exposure prematurely age the skin, but skin cancer can, and does, happen. I used to have a beautiful tan, until my doctor told me I was very close to getting skin cancer—it can happen to *you*! It's one of the most common of all cancers, comprising one-sixth of all new cancer cases diagnosed annually. Yet approximately ninety-five percent can be cured with early detection.

Skin cancer can be caused by too much sun and is rarely seen in protected parts of the body, such as those your clothing covers. Normally, the lighter the complexion, the more likely skin cancer is to occur; dark complexions rarely get skin cancer. Studies have also shown that daily habits play a large part in the development of skin cancer. For instance, in the United States, where a driver's left side of the face is exposed to the sun, skin cancer is more common on that side.

Now that you know the seriousness of the condition, here are some tips for helping to prevent it:

- Keep sun exposure to a minimum, even when you're trying to get a tan. Fast tanning doesn't work—planned, gradual tanning does.
- Get into the habit of using a sunscreen. Many cosmetic companies are including sunscreens in their products today. For the most part, a sunscreen helps absorb ultraviolet light waves, which create the damage, before they get a chance to hit the skin.
- Also, during prolonged sun exposure at the beach or during sports, be sure to use a suntan lotion with the highest sun protection factor (SPF) possible. Something with a SPF of fifteen, for example, is probably best. It will allow you to stay in the sun fifteen times longer than if you were unprotected—without damaging your skin. That gives you more time for outdoor activities, without the worry!

CARING FOR YOUR SKIN TYPE

Cleansing your skin routinely is only part of keeping it beautiful. Cleansing it *properly* is just as important. To do that, you must know what skin type you have. Do you know what category you fall into? Most people don't; so if you're not sure, you have plenty of company.

54

Basically, there are three categories of skin: oily, dry, and combination. Not too many people have "normal" skin, since it's rare to have a flawless complexion. Besides, what *is* normal? It's a relative term. So I'll exclude that category from any detailed discussion. Since oily skin plagues most teenagers, I'll concentrate on it.

Oily skin simply means that the oil glands are working overtime and producing too much oil. Results of this overactivity are greasy, oily skin, pimples, blackheads, whiteheads—that overall "icky" feeling. Therefore, you want to degrease the skin by cleansing with a water-based product. If you have an *excessively* oily skin, use an oil-free cleanser. The difference between the two? A water-based product means that water has been added to the ingredients, even though there may still be some oil in the product. An oil-free product contains no oil of any kind in it. To determine whether something is water-based or oil-free, take a look at the ingredients. If the word "water" is listed, it's a water-based product. If it's an oil-free product, oil will probably not be listed among the ingredients, nor anything associated with oil, such as eucalyptus oil, etc.

Basically, with an oily skin, you want to stay away from any thick, greasy creams or lotions, as they will only add to your problem. The word to remember here is dry. Instead, use products that are more watery in appearance and texture. If in doubt, look at the ingredients and note the appearance of the product before buying it. If there's a tester nearby, feel the texture of the product, keeping your eyes closed so you can concentrate better.

By the way, you can use this same cleanser on your face both before you apply makeup in the morning and when you want to remove it later on. When removing eye makeup, be sure to use a less drying cleanser. *This* is where a creamy product can be used, as you'll want to keep that area soft and prevent wrinkles from showing as much. If you have very sensitive eyes, you may want to use a watery, hypo-allergenic eye-makeup remover. And make sure you remove your eye makeup *gently*—your eyes are valuable!

That's all you really need to do for an oily skin. As for using a moisturizer, which helps to retain water, it is not necessary because your skin is producing all the moisture it needs.

In addition to using the right cleanser on your face, here are a few more tips for controlling oily skin:

- Keep your hair clean and off your face so you won't transfer oil to your complexion.
- Watch your diet, make sure you stay away from greasy, highly seasoned foods since they may provoke oil production, especially if you're allergic to them. Although it hasn't been proven that some foods, such as chocolate, are directly related to pimples, people who are allergic to them are certainly affected. If you have very oily skin, try not to eat as many dairy products—they usually have a very high fat content.
- Exercise regularly. It's good for your figure, too!
- Get a *moderate* amount of sunshine. This will give your skin healthy-looking color and camouflage flare-ups.
- Most important, *keep your hands off your face.* Just think of all the surfaces your hands touch between washings; if you cup your face with dirty hands, you may find yourself with more pimples in that *exact* area.

As I mentioned earlier, if you have oily skin, you should

56

cleanse your face three times a day. If you can't wash midday, cut up white wrapping tissue into small squares and use these "linen blotters" to soak up excess oil and makeup during the daytime. Or, if you prefer, you can buy commercially made blotters in some drug stores.

Generally, people with oily skin have a problem with acne. By definition, acne is a skin disorder marked by blackheads, whiteheads, pimples, and other lesions. Most oily skins have one or all of these conditions to some degree. However, sometimes the inflammation of the skin may be very serious, possibly causing scarring. But with proper care, the major scarring normally associated with a bad case of acne can be prevented. Don't be afraid to consult a dermatologist about any skin problems you may have. Your problems may be more severe than what simple cleansing can control, and a doctor may be able to help. When I was a teenager I developed a severe case of acne but was so scared that I put off going to a dermatologist. I finally did when my skin got very bad, and I have never regretted it.

No matter what, never pick at your skin to remove whiteheads, etc. Without proper dermatologic instruments, this picking can lead to scarring. Deep scarring usually occurs in the dermis, the second layer of the skin. The epidermis, the outside layer, rebuilds itself. The dermis usually doesn't. Therefore, superficial scars usually disappear when the skin cells rebuild a new layer of skin. The only way to get rid of deep scarring, however, is through surgery, and that's not always entirely effective. There is one procedure, called "dermabrasion," that consists of using an electric instrument, wire, or other abrasive tool on the skin. Once the procedure is completed, the patient's face is covered with dressings. When they are removed a week or so later, there are less scars.

I don't know about you, but I'd rather let a pimple take its time to disappear than risk scarring. After all, it generally takes only a *few days* for a pimple to go away. While you're waiting it out, try bringing attention away from a pimple by making up your eyes, or wearing your hair a new way.

The second category, *dry skin,* is just the opposite of oily skin. The oil glands are not producing enough oil. Results of this are a constant feeling of chapping and dryness. Unfortunately, if you have dry skin, it's probably something you were born with so, instead of trying to change it, you should learn how to control it.

Unlike oily skin, with dry skin you'll need to use an oil-based product to cleanse your skin (make sure you see the word oil in the ingredients). Use creams and oils—anything that adds and holds *moisture* back in your skin. That's the word to remember here. There are many products on the market that will do the job for you. You can find them in the cosmetic section of a department or drug store, and even in some grocery stores.

One nice thing about dry skin is that you won't have the acne problem that someone with oily skin does, although occasionally dry skin does break out. You might experience a condition known as contact dermatitis—usually nothing more than a reaction to a product you used on your skin. Since dry skin can be very sensitive, this is very common. Therefore, it is even more important to use a product that's unscented; it will irritate your skin less.

Another nice thing about dry skin is that your cleansing products can be used to remove your face and eye makeup, too, so you'll save money!

Since effective skin care gives the best natural look, distinguish my skin type & do the following:

○ I probably have dry skin, or combination skin.

(i) clean my face

(ii) Use a moisturizer, an unscented one

(iii) use a circular motion to massage my face

58

Unlike oily skin, a moisturizer is a *must* for dry skin, and an extra slathering is important when you brave chilly weather. Any moisturizer will do the job, but try to get a product that has mineral oil in it. It's great for a dry, thirsty skin! One word of caution, though: Since mineral oil can be rather heavy, if your skin is sensitive and starts breaking out, you may want to use a lighter, less clogging moisturizer without mineral oil or lanolin in it.

The third category, *combination skin,* is just what the name implies: part of the skin is oily and part of it's dry. Usually, most combination skins have an oily T-zone—forehead, nose, and chin (forming a *T*), although it's perfectly normal to have a different oily-dry combination.

I know it may sound time-consuming, but if you have this skin type you're going to have to use two different types of products on your skin—an oily skin cleanser for the oily sections, and a dry skin cleanser on the dry skin.

Unfortunately, in most cases, there is no one product that's *entirely* effective for cleansing a combination skin. Remember, you have two different types of skin to deal with, so you have to cleanse both areas differently. There is one exception, though: If your skin isn't *excessively* oily and dry, you may want to use something designated for normal skin, as long as it's not too drying or oily. Caution: Although it may seem obvious, if you do use two different kinds of products, don't get the oily skin product on your dry skin areas and vice versa. It'll defeat the whole purpose. Be sure to use a moisturizer on the dry areas of your skin, being careful not to apply it on your oily sections.

I know this may all be new to you and might be a bit confusing, so, to review, here's a chart that will help.

COMPLEXION CARE

OILY	DRY	COMBINATION
Cleanse 2-3 times daily with water-based or oil-free cleanser	Cleanse 2 times daily with oil-based cleanser	Cleanse 2-3 times daily
		Oily Sections: water-based or oil-free cleanser
		Dry sections: oil-based cleanser
No moisturizer	Moisturize	Moisturize *dry* areas only

I promised earlier that I'd cover masking more thoroughly. Although I don't feel it is absolutely necessary, used properly, a mask does refine the pores and gives your skin a smoother look, at least temporarily. Plus, it makes you feel good! However, like anything else you use on your skin, it's important to choose the right type of mask for your skin type.

For oily complexions, I'd recommend using a clay mask—because clay tightens a bit as it dries and absorbs excess oils. To determine if a mask is a clay one, look at the label. Most of them will have the word clay in the description. If it doesn't and you haven't been able to find a clay mask elsewhere, use a mask especially designed for oily skin instead. Remember

60

to avoid a product to which fragrance has been added or you may be defeating the entire process—fragrance can irritate *any* kind of skin. And especially avoid one that has a creamy feeling to it—you want to *dry* out your oily skin, remember?

On the other hand, for dry skin you'll need to use a mask that *is* creamy. Since a mask for dry skin won't contain any clay, it will not tighten as much as one for an oily skin. Again, make sure you don't use one with a fragrance added.

If you have a combination skin, for best results you'll need to use two different types of masks: a clay one on the oily areas and a moisturizing kind on the dry areas. If you aren't *excessively* oily, try one that's especially designed for normal skin.

YOUR OTHER COMPLEXION

Other than the skin on your face, you have another complexion—your body's. This is usually a bit different, especially if you have oily skin on your face.

Since you have no oil glands on the palms of your hands or the soles of your feet, and few on the top of your hands and elbows, this may account for the dryness you feel, and the need to moisturize often. Be sure to bathe or shower thoroughly in lukewarm water. You may want to use a loofah on some areas, too. It helps your blood circulate, and your skin will look and feel healthy and invigorated. If you use bath oil or take bubble baths, rinse thoroughly, as these substances might irritate your sensitive vaginal tissues. Use a mild soap, pat yourself dry, and apply hand lotion on the dry skin areas. Then, use an underarm antiperspirant/deodorant (antiperspirant helps stop wetness, deodorant helps stop odor) and you're finished.

You may want to insure freshness by applying baby powder all over your body, especially to your underarm area—it really gives you that confident feeling on those busy days.

If you have oily skin on your face, you probably are prone to oily skin on your shoulders and back, too. I'd suggest using the products you use to cleanse your face here, as well, and keeping any lotion off these areas.

DO I NEED MAKEUP?

This is probably something you've asked yourself dozens of times! Too often, we feel the pressure to do something, like wear makeup, without ever asking ourselves why, or *if* we want to! To answer that question for yourself, here's something to think about: If you can get away without it, great—you're lucky. But truthfully, *can* you?

To help find out if you really need makeup every day, or, for that matter, at all, do this. First, clean your face with the right cleanser until it's spanking clean, pull back your hair, and take a close look at yourself in a mirror (make sure you're in a well-lit room). Then take out a piece of paper and write down the answers to these questions:

1. Your personality and tastes: Do you like to wear makeup? If so, when? On what parts of your face? If you don't like to wear makeup, why not?

2. Your eye color: What color are your eyes—green, brown, hazel (changes to green or brown at different times), blue, gray?

3. Your eye definition: Are your eyes expressive, large, plain, or small? Are your eyelids droopy or puffy?

4. Your brows: Are they well-shaped, too bushy, or too skimpy?

5. Your skin condition: Is your skin clear or broken out?

6. Dark circles under your eyes: Do you have them?

7. Amount of cheek color: Is the natural color on your cheeks just right or are you too pale? Or, do you have too much color in your cheeks?

8. Your face shape: Is the width of your face too narrow, too wide, or just right?

9. Your lip color: Do you have just enough color on your lips naturally or are they too pale?

Once you've finished, go back and analyze your answers, keeping these points in mind: if you answered that you don't like to wear makeup, then, by all means, don't feel you have to all the time. However, remember you may *need* to! If this is the case, I'd suggest reserving it for special occasions. For example, I don't like to wear any makeup at home, but when I'm out teaching, I usually put on a little eye and lip makeup.

Everyone has limitations—what are yours? Remember that makeup can do great things for you, *if* it's applied correctly. Many people don't like makeup simply because they've seen it worn incorrectly on other people. So give it a chance before making any permanent decisions. It can give you a special look that spells CONFIDENCE. It'll add color and reshape any part of your face you'd like. Plus, it can make you look as many different ways as you want to.

Now for your specific features. What color are your eyes? What do they look like? Generally, if your eyes have a lot of color in them and they're large and expressive, you don't need much eye makeup. However, if they are not too color-ful, plain looking, and small, you're going to need more eye makeup to bring them out. The same goes for eye lids that are droopy or puffy, too, except that here you'll need to use some optical illusions in your makeup to make them appear less so —I'll go into that later.

If your brows are too bushy and could use some shaping, you're probably going to have to reshape them (more on this on pages 72-74). However, if they're too skimpy, usually due to overtweezing, you'll need to grow them out first. They're going to look funny for awhile, but overtweezed brows look even funnier! Unfortunately, there aren't too many things you can do to disguise brows while they're growing out—at least solutions I'd suggest. You can use an eyebrow pencil; but, frankly, even if you use a color that matches your brows and apply it with short, wispy motions instead of drawing it on, I still think the brows will look fake. Instead—and this applies to brows that are too skimpy or light-colored naturally —I'd suggest wearing an eye-catching accessory such as a necklace or pin. This will draw people's attention away from that area, and they'll probably not even notice your brows.

If you are very unhappy about your naturally light brows, the only other thing I'd suggest is to have them dyed professionally by a hair colorist. Never try to do something like this yourself at home; it takes a trained specialist to match your brow color with your hair coloring. Remember, however, that if you start dyeing your brows, the results will be only temporary and you will have to keep doing them.

How's the condition of your skin? I discussed this in the last section, but it bears repeating. If your skin is broken out, draw attention away from it by emphasizing your eyes more, dressing in something that makes you look terrific—anything to bring attention away from the negative.

If you answered yes to having dark circles under your eyes, you're probably going to have to use a concealer to help cover them. Other than lack of sleep or improper diet, dark circles can be hereditary. Also, as you get older, the skin around your eyes gets thinner and more transparent. This allows the bone

64

to show through more, which gives you the appearance of dark circles.

Look at the amount of color you have in your cheeks. If you're rather pale, you'll probably need to use blush; if you already have a lot of color, you're lucky—you don't need to wear blush!

For now, just keep the answer to question number 8 in mind. We'll get into applying makeup for your particular face shape later in the chapter.

Finally, how much color do your lips have? If they're a little pale, use a gloss or lipstick to add color.

All of this information should give you a better idea of whether you need makeup or not, and if so, where you need to apply it.

GETTING READY

Don't worry—you'll begin to apply makeup soon! However, you can't just put it on without some preparation beforehand.

- Always start with a clean face—putting makeup on a less-than-clean face will only make you look messy. Plus, it's not very good for your skin.
- Make sure you apply your makeup in good lighting. If the lights are dim, you may end up applying too much, and will look as if you're getting ready for Halloween instead!
- When you apply makeup, always begin with a little and add more as you need it. This is much easier than having to start all over again when you put on too much.
- Whatever makeup you apply, be sure to blend it in *thoroughly*—very important!
- After you've finished using your makeup, be sure to wash

the applicators. This prevents buildup and insures a smooth, professional look. If you don't have the time to wash applicators, try using cotton swabs, at least for your eye makeup, instead.

Now that we have a few basics down, you're *almost* ready to apply makeup, so gather up the following items if they apply to you. (If you don't have everything I suggest, use what you do have for now and purchase what you need when you can.)

- A medium-sized, stand-up mirror.
- Tissues.
- Cosmetic applicators—such as cotton swabs, brushes, etc. As far as what kind of brushes to get, it will depend on what follows. For example, if you use the powder form of blush, you will need a good brush. Most compacts have them. If you'll use lipstick instead of lip gloss, you will need a lipstick brush. I like the kind that retracts into its own case, but whichever one you feel comfortable with is fine.
- Eyeshadow (if you need eye makeup)—if you have oily lids, get the powder kind. Even people with dry or combination skin can have a problem with oily lids. As far as what colors to use, for a warm-toned complexion, try light brown, dark brown, *and* yellow. (Yes, yellow! Since you have a yellow base to your complexion, it will look natural.) If you'd like more color to your makeup, you may want to substitute peach for the light brown. For a cool-toned complexion, choose any pastel color you like as long as it's cool-toned, plus a gray *and* a pink.

No matter what color eyes you have, you'll find these

color choices will harmonize with your *entire* look. Selecting colors on the basis of just one part of you, like your eyes, isn't really doing you justice. As I mentioned earlier, others look at *all* of you, not part of you! (If you're still not sure whether you are warm- or cool-toned, go back to the section on color on page 32 for review.)

- Two clean toothbrushes, or a brow-lash comb.

- Mascara—be sure it matches the color of your own lashes.

- Cover-up and foundation (if you have dark circles under your eyes)—both of these should match your skin color. Make sure your foundation is an oil-based one, as you'll be applying it to your under-eye area only and that will need as much softening as possible, no matter what type of complexion you have.

- Blusher (if you need color on your cheeks, or have a narrow or wide face)—if you have oily skin, be sure to get the powder or gel type. For dry skin, the cream type is best. And if you have a combination complexion, either a type for oily or dry skin, depending upon how oily or dry your cheeks are. Regarding what color to use, for a warm-toned complexion, get something in the brown or peach families; for a cool-toned complexion, a pink or red.

Again, with the color you select for blush or for any type of makeup you wear, you're not trying to match your makeup to the clothing you wear. Rather, what you're creating is a "total look"—your makeup should complement the colors you're wearing in your clothing. In other words, if you have a warm-toned complexion, you'll wear warm-toned colors in your makeup *and* clothing; for a cool-toned complexion, vice versa.

- Lipgloss or lipstick: (if you need color on your lips)—if

67

you need just a little bit of color, a lipgloss will probably do. However, if you're really pale, you'll probably need lipstick. As for color choices, warm-toned complexions should wear something in the brown or peach families; cool-toned complexions would do well with a pink or red.

PUTTING IT ON

Applying makeup is a surprisingly simple skill to learn, but it does take some practice. Remember, none of us, not even professionals, were born makeup artists; so be patient.

To see for yourself how fast you'll progress, you may want to apply makeup to half of your face first, then make up the other side afterward—you'll probably see quite an improvement the second time around.

Since the best way of learning something new is by *doing* it, I'd suggest that you read each step and try it on yourself before going on to the next step. The procedure I'm presenting is for daytime makeup. You can change the order if you'd like since there's certainly no such thing as the one and only makeup technique. My method is simple, so if you're already using makeup, you'll learn how to do it even quicker! If a particular step doesn't apply to you, skip it and go on to the next one.

So, with all that behind us, shall we begin?

I always like to start with the *eyes*—they're the most fun to do, and since that's what others usually look at first, I think it's a good beginning.

The first step in applying eye makeup is what I call "the base step." With your light brown color (for warm-toned complexions) or a cool-colored pastel of your choice (for cool-toned complexions), apply shadow on your upper lid, up to the crease line.

See, wasn't that easy? You've just completed the hardest part—the beginning!

The next step is "the contour step." This is when the eyes start changing their shape, and you can really see the difference! Apply your shadow above the base step and into your skin (warm-tones: dark brown; cool-tones: gray) along your crease line, gradually going upward. Admittedly, this step is the hardest at first and usually takes the longest to get the hang of, but practice makes perfect. The key point to remember here is to apply your shadow *gradually,* not abruptly, upward and to *blend,* starting with a little, adding as you need it. If your eyelids are puffy, try taking the entire contour color up a bit higher. This will help make your eyes look less so. If you are Oriental, you may not have a distinct contour to your upper lids. In that case, you'll have to draw on a crease. To do that, simply apply the contour shadow the same way as previously discussed but make sure you blend it in extra well so it doesn't look drawn on.

If your eyes are very narrow looking and situated straight across in your eye sockets, you may want to try creating an optical illusion by angling the contour color up a bit more. Although you don't want to angle it up too much—it will look too unnatural that way—by angling it up a bit higher, your eyes won't look quite as straight on. Remember, any time you angle something, it looks more interesting, and that's what you're after here.

If your eyes are plain or small, you're going to want to use a *bit* more makeup (this goes for *all* eye makeup, including mascara, liner, etc.), going a bit heavier, but not too much. This will bring out your eyes more. Also, if your eyes tend to

The base step.

The contour step.

69

The highlight step.

droop, and many people's do, the upward direction of the contour step should give a nice optical illusion, making your droopy eyes appear more tilted in the other direction.

Next step is the highlight step. It's great for setting the whole look off and for blending all the layers together. Take your shadow (yellow for warm-toned; pink for cool-toned) and apply it on your browbone, where you don't have any shadow yet. Blend inward and downward, and there, you've just finished applying your eyeshadow!

To get rid of any shadow dust that might have collected on your brows and lashes, use one of your toothbrushes to brush off this debris—you'll look super-professional!

The next step is mascara, and does it make a big difference!

Instead of using the traditional technique of applying mascara from the base of the lash to the tip, I've found a better way. It will make your eyes look larger. Take your mascara and apply it on the *tips* of your top lashes only, going back and forth. To prevent any mascara clumps from drying, use your second toothbrush to remove clumps, without taking any mascara off. (*Don't* use a straight pin or anything like it to separate lashes. It's too dangerous and your eyesight is priceless. Plus, a too perfect look appears unnatural.) To balance out your look, you'll need to apply mascara on your bottom lashes, too, using the same technique.

If you find that your mascara is falling on your cheeks a few hours after application, it's probably the kind of mascara you're using, not the technique. Some mascaras have lash extenders built into them, so when you apply the mascara, your lashes look longer. However, gravity takes over and the extenders eventually start falling off. Your best bet is to use a regular formula for daytime, reserving the other kind for a special night out, when you'll be wearing your makeup for a shorter time.

Before leaving the subject of eyelashes, I'd like to discuss eyelash curlers. Don't use them on a regular basis. Every now and then is fine; but used regularly, they apply too much pressure on your delicate lashes, and you might lose a few. Unfortunately, there are few alternatives, so you will probably just have to accept your straight lashes and use eyelash curlers only occasionally.

Once your mascara is applied, the next step is eyeliner. There are several products you can use, but the technique I suggest using and will describe first is a money-saving one. Instead of using a product designated as eyeliner, you can use eyeshadow *for* eyeliner. Here's how.

Get a cotton swab and apply the color you used for the contour step (warm-tones, dark brown; cool-tones, gray). You'll be working on the under side of your lower lashes, not inside the rim of the bottom lashes near your eyeball (it may be in fashion, but applying makeup this close to your eyeball increases the chance of infection). Apply it in as thin a line as possible (you may want to remove excess cotton and twist to a point so you'll get a thin line), thicker on the outside corner, going thinner as you get to the inner corner of your eye.

Then, to balance out your new look and make your eyes appear as large as possible, apply the same color on the outer section of your top lid directly over the lighter shadow you originally used—the base step—going up to the crease line. It will really add depth. You're not drawing a line; rather, you're covering an *area.* Depending upon your features, you may find it too heavy for daytime and may want to reserve it for special occasions, instead.

The eyeliner step — for the lower lids . . .

and the upper ones.

If you prefer, you can use actual eyeliner instead of the eyeshadow technique I suggested. However, remember to use a color that blends in with your lashes so they will look natural. Line the entire base of your top lashes, making sure you line your lower lashes, too, for balance (use as thin a line as possible on both upper and lower lashes).

There are several types of liners on the market. Here's a rundown of what effect you will get from each kind.

A *crayon* eyeliner will give results that are very similar to that of my eyeshadow technique: a natural, "smudged" look. However, because crayons do have a high wax content, the liner usually doesn't stay on too long, so you're going to have to apply it more often.

A *liquid* eyeliner will create a clear, vivid look, but can be hard to apply. It takes a lot of practice *and* a steady hand. Once you master the technique, be sure to smudge in the line with your fingertip while it's wet, so it won't look as if it's drawn on. Caution: Make sure the liner is dry before opening your eyes wide or else you'll get the liner on your browbone.

Cake eyeliner is usually easier to use than a liquid eyeliner. All you have to do is dip the brush in water and apply. That's it! However, this type of liner usually won't create as clear a look as the liquid does.

Finally, the *pencil* liner. It's a bit harsh, because of the sharp point, so turn the pencil on its side and apply that way. The results are quite nice, but be sure to smudge the line with your fingertip so it won't look drawn on.

The next step is your *eyebrows.* Your eyes won't look their very best if your brows aren't shaped for your face. Whether nature gave you beautiful brows or not, a nicely shaped brow will help frame your eyes—it adds a finishing touch. It will also make putting on eyeshadow a lot easier and your eyes will appear larger. Too, since we communicate a lot through our eyes, if your brows are too bushy or skimpy, you may be communicating a harsh look even though you're not a harsh person.

To find out if your brows are correctly shaped for your face, look directly into your mirror, making sure your chin is parallel to the floor. Align the side of a straightedge, a pencil, or the bottom section of your toothbrush next to the side of your nose along the inner corner of your eye. The inner part of your eyebrow should begin where the edge ends.

If you have close-set eyes (eyes that are closer than the measurement of one eye apart), let your brows grow a bit farther apart from each other. It will create an optical illusion of width. If your eyes are wide-set (eyes that are farther apart than the measurement of one eye), grow your brows closer together, to create an optical illusion of closeness.

Creating optical illusions for close-set eyes (left) *and wide-set* (right).

73

To give your eyes more personality, it's important that your brows have an arch—a point that they *gradually* grow up to and then grow down from.

To find out where your arch should be, continue looking straight ahead into your mirror, chin parallel to the floor, and place your straightedge along the side of your nose and the edge of the iris of your eye. Your brow should arch at the point where the straightedge crosses your eyebrow, as in the first illustration below.

Next, to make sure your brows don't grow too far past the outer corner of your eye, take your straightedge once again, and, with your chin parallel to the floor, place it on the side of your nose and the outer end of your eye—your brow should end where it ends. (See the second illustration.)

Finally, it's important that your brows balance from every angle. To find out if yours do, take your straightedge and place it on the bottom ends of your brows, as in the third illustration, making sure they're even.

If you've now found that you need to reshape your brows, there are several methods available.

The first one is *tweezing.* I'll be honest with you: If you've never tweezed your brows before, it can be very tricky until you get used to it, as both eyebrows have to look the same. It may also hurt slightly. And it has to be done regularly, or you'll have lots of little stubbles growing in. However, it really is easy to do, once you have the hang of it.

Here are some tips to keep in mind:

- Always start with a just-washed face, and don't put lotion between your brows, especially if you have oily skin. Plus, you don't want the tweezers slipping.
- Be sure to sterilize your tweezers with hot water and alcohol—you might be opening up your freshly tweezed skin to bacteria if you don't.
- If you find that tweezing hurts a bit at first, place an ice cube on the area you'll be working on; it temporarily freezes the skin, and you won't feel the discomfort as much.
- Pull each stray quickly and in the direction it grows. Prolonging it and pulling in another direction will only hurt more—remember when you removed a bandage slowly from your skin when you were a little girl?
- Be sure to give yourself plenty of time. It won't take that long, but you don't need any extra pressure.
- Finally, reward yourself for good behavior—treat yourself to frequent breaks, listen to your favorite music. Be good to yourself! Believe it or not, it's not torture.

If you're not comfortable tweezing your brows yourself, don't despair—there are professionals who will do it for you.

Some salons provide this service quite inexpensively. Plus, that way you'll have it done correctly the first time, and you can take it from there yourself.

Another method of removing hair is *electrolysis.* You'll be happy to know that the procedure is permanent, but must be done by a highly trained professional called an electrologist. You should also be aware of some facts. First of all, depending upon how much hair you want removed (an electrologist can work on areas other than your brows), it usually takes a long time to complete the job. Using an electric needle to remove superfluous hair, an electrologist works on each hair individually and there are usually many hairs that need to be removed. Therefore, it can be rather expensive. Also, some people have found the procedure to be painful, although today many electrologists use a topical spray to help numb the area they'll be working on. As you can see, electrolysis is a definite commitment, so you'll need to be serious about it before you begin. Naturally, you can stop going at any point; but then, you'll be back to removing unwanted hair yourself again.

To find an electrologist, either have one recommended to you, or take a look in the *Yellow Pages* of your telephone directory. I'd also recommend taking advantage of their complimentary consultation before making a final decision. It's the easiest and least expensive way to find out if electrolysis is really for you.

While we're on the subject, I want to caution you to beware of the "permanent hair removal" equipment you can purchase from ads in various magazines. It takes a highly trained expert to use them properly. So it is best to leave this up to a professional.

The last alternative for hair removal is *waxing.* Done by a professional cosmetologist, the result, while not permanent, will discourage hair growth for up to six weeks, in most cases. Waxing is also inexpensive and painless!

Whichever brow-shaping method you decide to use, *don't* shave your brows—you don't have as much control with a razor. Also, *don't* use chemical hair removers, such as those safely used on the legs. The chemicals are much too harsh for the skin on your face, and your hand could slip, possibly causing blindness. Remember, your eyesight is priceless.

The next step in applying makeup is tending to your *dark undereye circles.*

To draw attention away from them, use your cover-up, gently dotting it on the darkened area. Don't rub in all the way, as the consistency usually doesn't allow this and it will look a bit cakey if you do.

To insure smoothness, apply your foundation over your cover-up. If you'd like to wear foundation over your entire face, see "For Those Special Occasions" at the end of this chapter for a more thorough discussion. While you won't be eliminating your dark circles entirely, it'll help to disguise them—and every little bit helps!

The next step in applying makeup is *blush.* Available in three forms, each one is designed for a particular skin type.

Powder blush is great for oily skin. Plus, it doesn't clog your pores as much. However, since it is applied on the top of your skin, it won't be quite as natural looking, so you may want to reserve it for evenings out instead.

The next form, *cream,* is great for dry skin because it is oil-based, but not so good for oily skin, as you can imagine. Also, it blends in beautifully on dry skin.

The third form of blush is *gel.* Since it is water-based, it's great for oily complexions. However, unless you know how to use it, it can be tricky. The major problem most people have with a gel blush is that it blotches. Because the product contains quite a bit of water, it will evaporate fast when it comes into contact with the air. So, be sure to blend it in as soon as you squeeze it out of the tube.

Select the right form of blush for you, remembering that for a warm-toned complexion, you should wear something in the brown or peach families, and for a cool-toned complexion, a pink or red-colored blush is best. Before you apply your blush, close your eyes and feel your cheekbones with your fingertips. Get to know them, because quite a bit of makeup application relates directly to your bone structure. Then, pay particular attention to the very top of your cheekbone. This is where you're going to apply your blush in three dots, approximately half an inch apart. Then, blend upward and around, forming a sideways *V.* Be sure to take your blush into your hairline so you won't have a false demarcation line.

If you have a narrow face, blend the *V* narrower, to give

Form a sideways V *with your blush* (left). *The* V *should be narrower for a thin face* (center), *and wider to slim a wide face* (right).

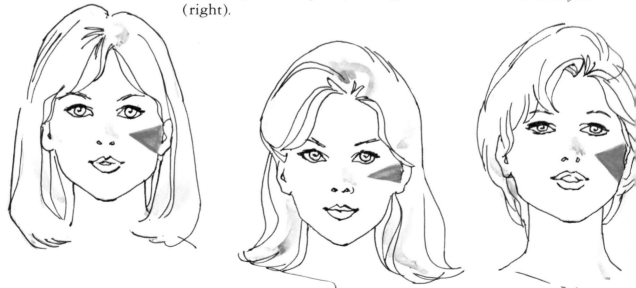

an illusion of width. If you have a wide face, take the *V* lower than your earlobe, to help slim.

The last step in applying makeup will balance out your whole new look: *lip color.*

Whether you use lipgloss or lipstick, select the right color: a brown or peach for a warm-toned complexion, a pink or red for a cool-toned complexion. Lip color is something, too, that should blend in with your outfit more than with any other makeup, as your lips are located closer to your clothing. For example, if you're wearing a lot of red, you're going to have to match the red in your lipstick almost exactly. Otherwise, it will clash. As far as how to apply lip color, if you like to use a gloss, simply apply it on both your top and bottom lips. However, if you use lipstick, I'd suggest using a lipbrush. It will help prevent your lipstick from "bleeding" outside your lipline, which can really look embarrassing! Also, you can use a lipstick pencil instead; but if you do, make sure you get a color that matches, or at least complements, your lipstick. In either case, here's how you do it: Line the outside of both your top and bottom lips with the pencil or a lipbrush (stroke the brush along the top of your lipstick to get some color). Then, fill in with your lipstick from the tube. To add some shine, you may want to top this with a gloss. That's all!

There—you've just completed the entire procedure! And it was easy, wasn't it? Remember, as you practice, you'll become better and better, and eventually, you'll find you can do it all in less than four minutes!

Now, take a look at the job you just did. The look you want to achieve is a natural extension of your own beauty. Makeup shouldn't be something that necessarily covers what you have. Rather it should *bring out* what you have. The colors, as well as the technique, should be pleasing to the eye, and shouldn't distract you or others. For example, have you ever noticed someone's makeup first, instead of the person? Probably. And you don't want that! When someone looks at you, they should see *you*— it should be difficult to see where the makeup starts, and *you* begin! Your makeup should not stick out like a sore thumb. They should all complement one another, especially where coloring is concerned; that's why it's important to wear warm-tones or cool-tones which, in turn, complement the same coloring in your clothing and accessories.

KEEPING IT ALL FRESH-LOOKING

As well made as cosmetics are today, it's impossible to keep your makeup looking fresh all day. That's because your skin secretes oil during the day, and this muddies up your look, especially if you have oily skin. Besides, regardless of the kind of complexion you have, makeup will eventually wear off. So, here are some tips that will make you look and feel your best:

- If you have oily skin, wash often during the day. Since you may not be able to, you might want to carry with you a small container of your cleanser and some cotton balls. If you can't do that or if you have dry skin and don't need to wash as often, use the blotters I spoke about earlier on page 57—they really help, believe me! Another alternative is to dust your face with dusting powder. It helps absorb excess oil. There are many kinds on the market (such as loose or pressed), and they come in many colors; but I would suggest using a translucent-colored powder so you can use it all year long.
- For that "crease grease" that collects in the crease of your eyelid, simply blot it up with a cotton swab.

80

- And, of course, especially if you have a long day ahead of you, you'll need to reapply your makeup every now and then, especially your eye makeup, blush, and lip color.

FOR THOSE SPECIAL OCCASIONS

Unlike daytime makeup, special occasion makeup is more dramatic, making use of darker colors. Dim lights have a tendency to steal color and definition from our features, so we have to compensate by adding more makeup. Also, special occasions are usually a time to dress up, and that includes dressing up our makeup, too!

As far as technique goes, it's almost the same as daytime makeup. However, there are a few differences.

First of all, you want to use darker colors, making sure you use the right coloring for your complexion, as always. In other words, instead of using a light brown or blue for the base step of your eye makeup, you'll want to use a darker brown or blue, for example.

In addition, although I don't think you need it, you may want to wear foundation all over your face. Foundation helps to blend all the different colors of your complexion into one. However, it's important that you get the right formula and shade for your skin type and coloring. Remember, if you have oily skin, you want to get a water-based formula (if you're excessively oily, an oil-free formula). For dry skin, use an oil-based one. And if you have a combination skin, choose something that is neither too oily nor dry. But if your skin tends toward one or the other extreme—mostly oily, use a product for oily skin; mostly dry, a dry-skin product.

As far as choosing the right color, I would recommend that you go to a well-stocked cosmetic counter barefaced and carry a small hand mirror. Ask the salesperson to show you as many foundations as possible for your skin type and coloring. Blend a small amount of foundation from each bottle onto separate sections of your jaw line. Since most stores have fluorescent lighting, which can be deceiving for color selection, walk to the nearest window and look at your face in the mirror, checking to see which foundation matches your skin color the best. If you can see where the foundation stops and bare skin begins, go back to the makeup counter and keep on trying. If not, then your choice is made!

To apply foundation all over your face, start by placing a dot on your forehead, nose, chin, and cheeks, then blending small areas at a time in a gentle, circular motion over your entire face, going into your hairline. (Use a damp cosmetic sponge to help blend.) After you've finished, check your makeup near a window to make sure you didn't miss any spots.

Occasionally, you may find that your foundation might have a chalky look to it. This could mean one of several things: your skin could be changing and probably needs a foundation with more moisture in it, or, if you're using old foundation, it may need to be replaced. The shelf-life for cosmetics is limited, so try not to keep products too long. To lengthen their life, screw the top on well.

OPTICAL-ILLUSION MAKEUP

Makeup can also be used to reshape your face by disguising your face shape, slimming your nose, etc.; but personally, I find this contouring and highlighting, as we call it, to be heavy-looking and not very natural. In fact, I don't recommend doing this at all unless you're going to have your picture taken.

82

Just in case you'd like to try it, though, here's how: Remember when we covered optical-illusion dressing in the wardrobe chapter, specifically, dark colors decreasing size and light colors increasing size? Well, the same concept is applied with contouring and highlighting your face. You can either contour under your foundation or over it, but take a close look at your unmade-up face first. Which areas would you like to be larger? Wider? Smaller? Narrower? On the areas you'd like to be larger or wider, you're going to apply a very light-colored foundation or highlighter. This step is called "highlighting." For example, if your nose is too narrow, then apply and blend in a small amount of light-colored makeup along the sides of your nose. Face too narrow? Apply your light-colored makeup along the sides of your face. Especially in a photograph, your face and nose will appear wider!

Now, for the areas you want to be smaller or narrower, use the same technique but this time use a very dark-colored foundation or blush. This is called "contouring." Is the tip of your nose too large, for instance? Dab and blend in a bit of your dark-colored make-up there. How about your face shape —too wide? Dot your dark-colored make-up along the sides of your face. You'll notice these areas immediately recede.

As you can see, the technique is easy, once you have the hang of it. But it can be very heavy-looking, so I feel it should be reserved for certain occasions only.

SINCE YOU ASKED . . .

I have an oily complexion and have been following your suggestions on cleansing oily skin. But how do I keep my skin soft? I don't want to use creams, as this will cause my skin to break out more.

Good for you for not breaking down by using creams! It's a temptation, but as you know, an oily skin needs no more oil.

Frankly, I can't suggest anything but time. Your skin will start to produce its own oil a couple of hours after cleansing. That might then give it a softer look. If you absolutely cannot stand it, and if you don't have an excessively oily skin, there are some very good oil-free moisturizers on the market now that you can use. But keep it to a minimum. Remember, you don't need more moisture!

If I clear up my oily skin condition, will the enlarged pores on my face disappear?

Unfortunately, no. Once your pores are stretched out of shape, it's impossible to shrink them back, at least permanently. If you want to temporarily make your pores appear smaller, you can use a mask on your face—the results will probably last a few hours.

Can I use a cover-up for my pimples?

Sure, as long as it's not oil-based. Remember that a pimple is usually caused by too much oil, among other reasons, so make sure you check that there is no oil listed in the ingredients. You might also try one of the medicated cover-ups on the market.

My mother won't let me wear mascara until I'm thirteen years old —I'm twelve—but all the kids at school wear it. What can I do?

Compromise! I'm sure your mother has a good reason for not letting you wear eye makeup right now. However, I recognize the importance of "fitting in." Why not put some petroleum jelly on your lashes to give your eyes a larger look? I'm sure your mother wouldn't mind that.

My lips are really small on top. What, if anything, can I do to make them appear larger-looking?

84

While there is one thing you can do, I'm not sure you're going to like doing it, as, in my opinion, your lips won't look very natural. But here goes: when applying your lipstick, you may want to draw your top lip a bit larger with a lipstick brush or lipstick pencil, filling in with your lipstick. In other words, you're basically drawing on thicker lips! It looks great for a while, but eventually, your "new" lip will wear off. This technique is best kept for when you have your picture taken. A compromise might be to line your top lip a *bit* larger instead of simply drawing on a new one. Remember, though, it's going to wear off, so you'll have to touch up very often.

I was just curious about something—with all the companies putting out products that eventually prove to be dangerous for consumers, is the cosmetic industry regulated by anyone?

Yes, it is. The Food and Drug Administration (FDA) is the governmental body responsible for regulating, at least partially, the cosmetics industry. However, remember, there are so many thousands of cosmetic companies in business that's it's hard to regulate everyone. I'd suggest you write the FDA and ask them to send you information explaining how cosmetics are regulated, new regulations protecting consumers, etc. Write: Consumer Commission Office, NJF-10, 5600 Fishers Lane, Rockville, MD 20857. You'll find it to be very enlightening, I'm sure!

I wear glasses all the time. Is there anything different I should know about eye makeup?

Yes, there certainly is. If you wear glasses, you're going to have to make up your eyes much darker because your lenses tend to reflect light, and this steals definition from your eyes. For example, I wear glasses part-time. When I know I will be wearing them, instead of using brown mascara and eyeliner, and light-colored eyeshadows, I go into black mascara and eyeliner, and darker shades of my favorite shadows.

I have very sensitive eyes, and I can't seem to find any *eye makeup that doesn't bother me. Since I want to wear eye makeup so badly, what do I do?*

If you have truly tried everything, including cosmetic lines especially designed for sensitive eyes, cosmetics your ophthalmologist or optometrist recommends, etc., then I'd suggest accepting it. At this point, it's a decision between looking terrific and feeling terrible, or looking not as terrific but feeling great. The answer's going to have to be whichever one you feel most comfortable with. One idea: Are you *sure* it's the makeup that's bothering you? And are you *applying* it correctly? I knew someone who used a powder eyeshadow, which dropped into her eyes constantly. I suggested she switch to a cream eyeshadow. Perhaps you may want to review your own procedures and the products you're using.

Do you have any suggestions for the contact-lens wearer? I find it hard to make up with the lenses in; yet, without them in I can't get a good overall picture of what I've done.

Yes, I agree—it can be a difficult situation! Happily, there *is* something you can do about it. If you wear soft lenses, this is probably not a problem, as they should be put in before making up. Otherwise, the lenses may touch the makeup and absorb it. However, if you wear hard lenses, you'll need to put them in after making up. Use a magnifying mirror especially designed for close work. Since there are so many people in this predicament, you'll probably be able to find a mirror such as this at your local drug or department store.

86

I'm black and have determined that since I have a lot of yellow to my complexion, I look best in the warm colors. However, every time I make myself up with all the browns, yellows, peaches, etc., I look "blah"—and my features don't stand out. What do you suggest?

In your case, while you want to bring out your natural coloring, you do need more of a contrast to bring out your features. Therefore, I'd suggest staying with the same warm colors but instead using the brighter, more vibrant versions of them. For example, instead of a skin-tone peach, you may want to go into a bright (but not light) peach. You're certainly right—makeup should blend in, but if it blends in too much, it's not doing its job!

No matter what I do, I seem to have little bumps on my face. I've tried everything, but nothing seems to work. I'm black, and I heard that blacks seem to have an oilier skin than others. What should I do?

Actually, people with black skin are no more prone to oilier complexions than light-skinned people. Are you using the right kind of cleansing products on your skin? If so, and the problem persists, I'd suggest seeking advice from a professional such as a dermatologist. These bumps may be nothing more than ingrown hairs, which your doctor can determine.

Goals := 1. Select a hairstyle which will balance my entire look

2. Enhance what I already have, bring out my best points, & camouflage some of my worse ones

Principle : Use the concept of optical - illusion dressing in p. 31,

STEP 5

the key is to have a hairstyle to balance factor #4 of the following :

YOUR CROWNING GLORY

○ 4 factors determine my hairstyle

1. My personality, or who I'm,

what hairstyle will express me or my lifestyle → ✓ 1. Sporty & active lifestyle. I love life & do things to enrich my life.

2. Professional

3. Entrepreneur or businessman,

2. The texture of my hair

{ Fine ✓ → short haircut

{ Medium

{ Thick

3. My body proportion → Average height with medium size → short hair, but NOT too short

4. The features of my face

(i) The bone structure of my face → Medium

< small face

< large face

(ii) The shape of my face → round face.

< narrow

< wide

(iii) The shape of my head :

Do I need to use a hairstyle to cover any imperfection or any natural growing process.

I'm bald → I want to have more volume on the top. → Do some layers

(iv). Any features of my face I want others to draw attention to or to avoid ?

○ It's important to shop around for a hairstylist. (p 103)

Y OUR HAIR *CAN* BE YOUR CROWN-ing glory, but like anything else, it reacts to the care that you give it. Most people just aren't lucky enough to be born with beautiful hair—they usually work for it.

Other than just working hard toward beautiful hair, it's also important *how* you work for it, and that's what this chapter is all about.

WHAT'S IN A HAIR?

Most people tend to take the hair on their head for granted. They wash it, dry it, style it, roll it, color it, etc., etc. But do you *really* know what your hair is all about?

On the average, there are about one hundred thousand hairs on the scalp, all within an area of about one hundred twenty square inches. The number of hairs on your head is genetically determined. Generally, redheads have the least

88

hairs, and blonds have the most. If you've ever worried about the hair you lose each day, don't; it's normal to lose around fifty to eighty scalp hairs daily. That's the only way old hair can make way for the new.

Hair is mostly protein, and each strand has three layers. The outer one, called the *cuticle,* contains overlapping cells resembling shingles and basically acts as a protector. The middle layer, or *cortex,* contains pigment and determines the color of the hair. As you get older, the production of pigment slows down and this accounts for gray hair. (Some people think gray hair is caused by stress, but that has not been proven.) The innermost layer, the marrow of hair, is called the *medulla.* This layer is sometimes absent in very fine hair and although its purpose is not exactly determined, many believe the medulla is a waste eliminator—an excellent cleansing mechanism for the body.

Hair is one of the fastest-growing tissues on the body, growing as much as one-half inch a month. However, as you get older, hair growth slows down, and the quality of hair becomes poorer; this is why children's hair is usually much more lustrous and beautiful. The average life of a hair ranges from two to four years, depending upon factors such as sex, age, hair type, heredity, health, nutrition, and hormonal activity. In addition, hair growth is influenced by the seasons of the year, growing faster in warm weather.

The basis for all hair growth is the papilla. About two months after conception in the womb, follicles (from which our hair grows) start forming. During childhood, a smooth down of hair called "vellus" covers the body; and right around the time of puberty, the body produces a coarser hair, called "terminal" hair. The follicles operate continuously for up to seven years, then shut down temporarily. Follicles are also responsible for producing the type of hair we have: straight, wavy, curly, or something in-between.

Tweezing has a tendency to stimulate follicles, which increases hair production. But, contrary to popular belief, shaving does *not* thicken hair! And natural body—the amount of thickness your hair has—is due in part to the diameter of your hair.

There's a lot to those little strands on your head, isn't there?

GETTING DOWN TO BASICS

Now that you have a better idea of what your hair is, let's get down to basics. As I mentioned before, many people have potentially beautiful hair but rarely see it. For the most part, this is because they use hair products that are wrong for their scalp and hair type.

Scalps fall into one of three categories: oily, dry, and normal. The scalp is where hair is manufactured and oil—either too much, not enough, or just the right amount—is produced. Most teenagers fall into the oily category, since this is a time when skins are oily, too. The oil glands underneath the scalp's surface produce too much oil, and as you'd expect, the result is greasy hair in need of frequent washing. Other contributing factors to an oily scalp are stress, hot climate, or hormonal changes within the body, such as menstruation. So, if you have oily hair, the last thing you want to use is a product that contains oil. Do *not* use products that feel very creamy to the touch. Also, products that list balsam as an ingredient should be avoided on a regular basis. They usually contain a paraffin (wax) base to coat the hair, attracting dust and dirt.

What to use? Try water-based hair products. These usually come in gel form and are great for degreasing your scalp. And, as with cosmetics for your skin, use the unscented version. Fragrances usually contain essential oils, and these will only make your hair oilier.

When shampooing your hair, concentrate the cleanser on your scalp and the base of your hair, where it's needed the most. Let the water you rinse with help take care of cleaning the rest of your hair. Why? Because hair grows from the scalp; the hair shafts are dead and dry out quickly as they get older. If you use a shampoo made to degrease oily hair on your ends, you may dry out your dry hair shafts more than necessary, possibly causing breakage.

To add moisture to your dry hair strands, especially those at the ends, conditioning is a must. You have two options: a water-based conditioner all over your head, or a rich, creamy type, applied to your hair strands only, not on your scalp. (If your hairstylist recommends using a creamy type all over your head because of your specific needs, make sure you rinse well.)

The second category, dry scalp, is the opposite of oily. As you know by now, a dry scalp means that not enough oil is being produced by your oil glands. Too, dry hair is often dry because it doesn't contain enough oil to retain the water that gives hair its suppleness. Hair loses its lustrous look because of this lack of moisture (hair is about 10% water). Dry hair is also caused by abuse—blow-drying, sun, drying shampoos, etc. Certain types of hair, such as thick, heavy hair, also have a tendency toward dryness.

Those with dry scalps don't experience the frustration of always having to shampoo because of greasiness. However, they have their share of worries, too. There's often a problem with flyaway hair; and they also sometimes experience dandruff—dry, flaky skin caused by a lack of moisture. Mostly,

91

like the person with dry skin, there's always a feeling of dryness, as if the hair needs to be moisturized often.

If you fall into this category, that's the word to remember —*moisture.* Use a shampoo that's loaded with oil and moisture on both your scalp and hair strands. And, after every shampoo, be sure to condition your hair with a rich, creamy conditioner. Massage it into your scalp and hair, leaving it on for a while while your head is towel-wrapped. Then rinse thoroughly, so you won't be left with any dulling residue.

A third, but rare, category is a normal scalp: neither too oily, nor too dry. Lucky you, you can get away with using just about anything on your hair (within reason, of course!). Make sure the hair products aren't too drying, however, because they might cause some breakage. Also, I'd suggest using a conditioner, at least on your ends. This will replenish moisture your hair is probably losing by your use of electrical appliances, as well as being in the sun. If you apply conditioner all over your head, be sure to rinse thoroughly.

Getting Ready for the Shampoo

As you've found out by now, you usually can't just go full force into any beauty routine until you've done a few things beforehand. This applies to shampooing your hair, too.

Start by massaging your entire head, working in small areas gently, with the pads (not nails) of your fingers. Not only does it feel wonderful, but it's good for you, too. Massaging increases circulation, bringing blood to feed your scalp. The result is healthier-looking hair.

Next, brush your hair to remove any tangles, as well as to give your scalp one more chance to get that blood circulating.

92

After all, it's the only exercise your scalp really gets, so give it a good, *gentle* workout. Start with your head bent over forward and brush downward, then change the position of your head by looking up toward the ceiling and brush back. Be sure to brush with long, flowing strokes—it'll help prevent split ends.

Last, wash your combs and brushes thoroughly, making sure you rinse well. It just doesn't make any sense to wash your hair, and then use soiled combs and brushes afterward.

Now you're ready to shampoo your hair!

The Shampoo

Now that you've relaxed yourself, detangled your hair, and cleaned your combs and brushes, get your shampoo out. With soaking wet hair, take a small amount of shampoo and work up a lather in the palm of your hand. Start by shampooing your scalp, using the same motions you used in the head massage. You're going to be shampooing at least once; but if you'd like to do it twice to be sure your hair is really clean, concentrate the first time on cleansing your scalp, the second time on cleaning your hair strands. Just clean the first few inches, since the ends won't normally need it as much. Plus, if you have an oily scalp, your shampoo might dry out the ends. If you have very oily hair, leave the suds on a few minutes before rinsing. It'll help clean your scalp even more.

Rinse your hair thoroughly. This will prevent any dulling soap residue from remaining. In fact, a lot of people think they have dandruff when it is really soap residue.

To find out if you've done a good rinse job, give yourself the "squeak" test. Going section by section, take a few strands of wet hair and pull them gently between your thumb and forefinger. If you hear a squeak in every area you test, you've probably rinsed the soap out thoroughly enough. If not, rinse again.

After your hair is rinsed of all shampoo, use your conditioner, as discussed in the last section. Ask your hairstylist how often to use it, as he or she knows your hair best. Or, follow product directions.

After the Shampoo

Too often, many people put lots of effort into shampooing but then neglect to carry that forward into what they do with their hair afterward. If you're not careful here, too, you may become a bit too aggressive with combs, etc., and damage your hair!

Start by combing your hair, beginning on the ends and work up to your scalp. If your hair is tangled, a large-toothed comb is best. This may take a bit longer than what you might have been doing, but you'll find the time a good investment. Pulling on tangles, instead of gentle removal, will guarantee breakage. Don't use a brush on wet hair. It tends to cause breakage.

YOU ARE WHAT YOU EAT

Yes, I know, you've probably heard that hundreds of times before, but once more certainly won't hurt—especially since you *are* what you eat!

If you eat irregularly and your diet includes junk food and too many sweets, chances are that unless you are very lucky it probably shows up in your hair. It also affects the rest of your appearance and your health, too.

No matter how many arguments you may come up with, none of them will stand up to the advice that's been handed

94

down for generations: Eat a well-balanced meal three times daily. Since more on diet and exercise is coming up in the next chapter, that's all I'll say for now.

TREAT YOUR HAIR LIKE CRYSTAL

You're probably wondering what on earth crystal has to do with hair, right? Well, if you've ever been to a crystal shop, you might have noticed all the DO NOT TOUCH signs scattered around the display area. They're there for good reason. Crystal is *very* delicate. The same is true of your hair. Although it's strong and is replaced by new hair, it is delicate and takes months to completely replace itself. Although hair grows at the rate of about one-half inch a month, that can feel like forever when you're trying to grow your hair out!

So, the first thing to remember is to use the proper tools— a sturdy comb, whose size you feel comfortable with, and a natural or boar-bristle brush. They prevent static electricity and give more control. They also help prevent breakage. Although a nylon-bristle brush is less expensive, firmer, and is more readily available, it can spell disaster for your hair if used regularly. It tends to be harsher on your hair and many people who use it complain of having flyaway hair. Your best bet is a natural bristle brush. It has baby-soft bristles that caress caress each strand, and although it's usually more expensive and may be harder to find, it will help keep your hair in the healthiest condition. To find one, try a brush company, a good department or drug store. There is, however, an alternative that offers a compromise—a boar-bristle brush. It's usually less expensive than the natural-bristle kind and can be found in many stores. In addition to the above, there are many other types of brushes on the market designed more for styling than for grooming. Ask your hairstylist to recommend one for

95

your needs—you may be able to get one brush that's not only good for brushing but styling, too.

Also, as I've discussed before, when combing or brushing your hair, don't snap your ends. Your hair is like crystal, remember? And, it will break if it's mistreated. Instead, use long, gliding motions, carrying your comb off your ends *gently.*

Be careful about what you put on your hair when styling it. For example, when putting your hair up with rubber bands, don't use the regular kind, such as those used to hold newspapers. They're not designed for hair and will probably break it if they are used regularly. Instead, get coated rubber bands (usually called ponytail holders). You'll really notice the difference. If you like to put fashion combs in your hair, that's all right. But if possible, hold the hair back loosely, not tightly, especially if you wear them often. Remember, the more you pull something, the looser it can become, so treat your hair gently!

Mechanical devices, such as blow dryers and electric hairsetters, can be damaging, but *only* if certain precautions aren't taken. Since we've all come to depend upon them so heavily, we should learn to work with them, instead of allowing them to work against our hair. You can counteract their drying effect by treating your hair especially nice. If you have oily hair, apply lots of conditioner on your ends after every shampoo. For dry hair, apply it all over your hair. The sun is also drying, so cover your head with a scarf or hat when sunbathing. Shampoo chlorine and salt out of your hair immediately after swimming (or at least rinse it); if you're coloring or perming your hair, take precautions over and beyond those that I've suggested above, as both processes can dry out your hair.

96

While I'm on the subject of coloring, let me pass on something for you to think about. When I was in junior high school, I thought about going blond, like everyone else at school. (I'm a brunette.) A good friend of mine at the time said, "Jane, if you were supposed to be a blond, you would have been born a blond!" Well, it took many years before I believed her, and, in the meantime, my stubborn nature won out—I eventually traded in my brown locks for blond ones. Sure, I felt that I looked glamorous and elegant, as long as I had the brown roots retouched often. But soon I found coloring to be expensive, time-consuming, and basically not worth it—not to mention never being quite sure if that was the best color for me.

When I got married, I finally decided to go back to my natural hair color, as an experiment and as a wedding gift to my husband, who hated my unnaturally blond hair. Reluctant at first because I didn't know whether others would treat me as they had when I was a blond, I found not only was I treated well, but even better! Plus, my natural color really did look a lot nicer. Moral of the story: If you must color your hair, that's fine; but make sure you *need* to and that it would be an improvement in your appearance.

Also, have a professional, whose specialty is color, do it. Many teenagers who are thinking about coloring their hair begin by experimenting with peroxide. Then they graduate to do-it-yourself home-coloring kits. That's not always the best route to take at first, especially if you don't know colors well enough (it *is* an art!). It may well be worth the extra investment to have your hair colored by a pro first. Many people end up with the wrong color by doing it themselves, and eventually have to go to a professional to have it corrected anyway. Plus, because hair is so delicate after being colored, if you want to change it, you cannot recolor it for a few weeks in order for the hair to "rest."

FINDING THE RIGHT HAIRSTYLE FOR YOU

Actually, the best hairstyle for you is not necessarily the one that is in style at the moment. Although that's important, selecting the best hairstyle is based upon much more than that. Here are some of the most important points to consider.

Like optical-illusion dressing, you're going to apply some of the same concepts to choosing a hairstyle, too. Using your bone structure and other considerations as guidelines, your goal is to select a hairstyle that will not only balance your entire look but will also enhance what you already have, bring out your best points, and camouflage some of your worst ones.

The first thing you need to look at is your bone structure, determining if your face is small or large. If you have a small face, your best bet is to choose a style that doesn't overwhelm you. That's where balance comes in. Too much fluff, or hair, will make your face appear even smaller. So it's better to stick with a style that is closer to your head.

This . . .

not this.

If your face is large, a shorter style with less hair will only make your face appear larger. Just compare these two hairstyles. Doesn't the one on the left look much better?

This . . .   *not this.*

② You also want to consider the shape of your face—whether it's narrow or wide. If your face is on the narrow side, a style that is midlength (to the chin), with volume and width on the sides, is probably best for you. In short, create a horizontal, instead of a vertical, look, and do not part your hair in the middle. Here are a couple of examples:

. . . or . . .

For a wide face, you need more length, less height, and less width. A middle part would work quite well for you:

If you're neither narrow nor wide, study the angles of your face: Where are the narrow parts? The wide parts? You can play down those areas with the proper hairstyle, too. For example, the style on the left would be great for someone with a wide forehead and narrow jawline. For someone with a narrow forehead and a wide jawline, the one on the right is best.

③ When selecting a hairstyle, another consideration is the shape of your head. Feel your head with both hands—get to know it. Where are the bumps, the dents? If there are some real imperfections, such as a dent on the crown of your head, wear a style that adds fluff and curl, or some type of height, in that area.

④ Also consider the texture of your hair, as well as the amount of wave and body you have before making a final choice. You may like a hairstyle, and it may look good on someone else, but it might not work for your hair. For example, if the texture of your hair is very fine, your hair will probably not lend itself to a long hairstyle. Otherwise, you'll end up very straggly looking, unless you perm it constantly. Your best bet is to select something that is shorter and layered—something that works *with* your hair, instead of *against* it. On the other hand, if your hair is excessively thick and wavy, and your bone structure allows you to do this, you may want to consider a longer hairstyle. The weight of your hair will help straighten and calm down your thick hair, and it'll probably be easier to manage than if it were short.

Your bone structure, face, and headshape are only part of what you should consider when selecting a hairstyle. The other part is *you*—your personality and tastes, as well as the image you want to project. Other people do make judgments about you, based on first impressions. So you want to make sure your hairstyle is "you," and not someone else! Why not put together a hairstyle image journal (similar to the one I suggested on page 28) to give yourself some specific clues?

It's also important to keep in mind how often you want to see your stylist for a cut. Regular trims will lengthen the life of your style and you really do have to stay on a regular schedule if you want to look your best. Many teenagers are afraid to have their hair cut, especially if they have long hair. However, even long hair needs shaping in order to give it that healthy look. Once split ends split, they keep on splitting up toward the scalp, so you're better off having your hair trimmed anyway.

Generally, the shorter the style, the more often you're going to have to have it trimmed. About every two to three weeks for short, layered hair—it loses shape that soon. For a longer style, about every six to eight weeks.

Still another consideration: How much do you want to care for your new style? In other words, do you want a wash-and-wear style; do you want to style it with a blow dryer; or do you want to use an electric hairsetter? Or can you use all three methods, depending on the occasion and your mood? The amount of time you're willing to spend on your hair has a lot to do with which style you select. A wash-and-wear style will take the least amount of time to care for. To make sure it stays in place, you may want to apply a styling gel to your wet hair, comb it in, and let it dry. If you're in a hurry and don't want to mess up your style by blow-drying, pick up a diffuser (you can find these at most beauty supply stores and some salons). It's an attachment you add to your dryer that helps dry your hair without resulting in a strong air flow.

A hairstyle requiring blow-styling will, of course, take a bit longer to style than a wash-and-wear one. Since blow-styling methods vary with each hairstyle, it's best to have your stylist show you how to do it for your particular look. However, here is one method that works well. Start by towel-drying the excess moisture out of your hair, because hair doesn't take its shape when soaking wet. Blow-dry the hair overall for a few minutes, just to make sure you get more moisture out. Then work section by section with your brush. Bring each section forward, wrapping it around your brush, dry it, then let the hair cool on the brush for a few minutes. Continue until you're finished styling. Blow-drying can be tricky and requires lots of practice, so be patient. To prevent dryness, always keep the dryer moving, and never allow it to stay in one area for too long.

If you prefer to use an electric hairsetter, the mist-type is probably best, as it helps feed moisture back into your hair. Designed to be used on your dry hair, these rollers can give more body to your hair, especially if you roll small sections at a time. They are time saving, as you merely put the rollers in your hair, wait until they're cool (while you're doing other things), and brush out to your favorite style. The exact setting pattern depends on the style you're aiming for, so again, check with your hairstylist.

You may also want to use a curling iron. It's designed to curl your hair quickly, and it's great for touch-ups. Work in small sections to get maximum coverage. And be sure to use a rich conditioner as often as possible since the dry heat will usually dry out your hair.

Remember, too, that different types of hair respond differently to methods of hairstyling. If your hair refuses to take a curl, a short cut that is blown dry is good, if you prefer a low-maintenance look. If you prefer more fullness with this type of hair, a roller set would be best, because it tends to hold better than a blow-styled or a curling-iron set.

FINDING A HAIRSTYLIST

There are many good hairstylists out there, but very often finding or changing hairstylists can be difficult because you not only have to find someone who specializes in what you o Good sh.

like and need but also who you feel comfortable with.

If you're shopping around, start by keeping your eyes open. When you see someone whose hair you like, ask who her stylist is. Yes, I know, you may find that embarrassing, but I think you'll find that she'll take it as a compliment!

While you're compiling your list, do the self-analysis I suggested earlier in this section: consider your bone structure, your face and head shape, your personal tastes, the image you want to project, and especially, how much time and money you're willing to invest in your hair. Also, collect photos of looks you like, as well as those you don't, so you can give your stylist the clearest idea possible of what you want.

Before you make an appointment to have your hair done, interview the stylists on your list. Call them up and explain that you're shopping for a new hairstylist and would like to schedule a few minutes of their time to speak with them about your needs before having anything done. Most will agree to do this hair consultation free of charge, but, for courtesy's sake, if you say a few minutes, *mean* a few minutes. They're probably very busy, and you certainly wouldn't want to be rude, especially when they're being kind enough to spend time with you.

Go over with them the information you've learned about yourself and show them your pictures. Spend a few minutes getting to know them, their background, and their specialties. Ask them what they'd do with your hair. Also, keep in mind how you feel with them—are you intimidated or can you communicate? If you can't, find someone you do feel good with. This stylist may be good, but your relationship with this person is important, and you should be comfortable.

After you're finished, thank them for their time, telling them you may be getting back to them. Then, on to the next stylist on your list, if you wish to continue your search. Remember, it's *your* hair! It may be a bit scary at first, because you've probably never done this before, but isn't it better to find out if they're the hairstylist for you before it's too late? However, if you liked that person, feel free to schedule an appointment—he or she is probably the one for you, and you'll be happy you went through all this.

SINCE YOU ASKED . . .

Does washing your hair every night ruin it?

Actually, it depends on what type of hair you have. For example, if you fall into the oily category, washing your hair every night, provided you use a shampoo designed for your hair-type, is fine because you have an excess of oil. However, as you can imagine, if you have dry hair, washing it every night would dry it out too much.

What should I do about hair that goes frizzy after washing?

Sounds to me like you've been blessed with naturally curly hair! If so, perhaps you're not using your blow dryer correctly. When blow-drying your hair, be sure to dry it until it's completely dry. Otherwise, your naturally curly hair will "go natural"! If you don't have natural curl, have you had your ends trimmed? And in either case, are you conditioning your hair regularly? Lack of moisture also causes frizzy hair.

Whenever I'm out in the rain or in humid weather, my hair gets frizzy, and it seems like the time I spend blow-styling my hair in the morning is wasted. What can I do?

Several things. You can try using a gel on your hair before drying it. With the extra weight, your hair wouldn't be quite as susceptible to frizzing once dried. Another solution, and the one I most recommend, is to accept what your hair does

105

and, instead of coaxing it to stay smooth, choose a hairstyle that looks fabulous even when it's frizzy. In other words, by having it cut properly, your hair will start working *for* you, instead of against you. It'll be a lot less frustrating, believe me —*I* used to fight the frizzies myself!

Is there anything wrong with brushing my hair when it's wet? Some people have told me there is, and other people have told me there isn't.

Actually, both sides are right. It's usually not advisable to brush wet hair, because wet hair is very vulnerable to damage. However, if you brush your hair with the *right brush,* there shouldn't be any problem. A regular hairbrush won't do, but a vent brush will work just fine. The bristles are spaced wide apart, and they are usually used when blow-drying hair. You can find vent brushes just about anywhere, but especially at your local beauty-supply store or many hair salons. You could also use a plastic wide-tooth comb, which will minimize breakage.

Do you suggest using hair spray? If so, which kind is the best?

Yes, I do, but quite a bit of whether or not you use hair spray depends upon how *you* feel about it. For example, some people don't like anything sprayed on their hair; others don't mind. There are some excellent hair sprays on the market, and all are designed to keep your hairstyle in place. Hair salons also carry good hair sprays, so you may want to check there, too. But remember, when you spray it on your hair, follow directions. Otherwise, your hair will end up very stiff looking, no matter how light the formula is. Also, when you wash your hair, be sure to do a thorough job of shampooing. You'll have a little bit more to remove from your hair, and you wouldn't want to be left with any residue afterward.

I'm black and I have kinky hair. If I use a straightener on it, it looks great, but I'm getting really tired of doing that. What else can I do?

You have two alternatives, as I see it: continue trying to change your hair texture, such as what you're doing, or do nothing about it. It's that simple. Since you obviously don't want to hassle with straightening your hair anymore, I'd suggest you get a hairstyle that complements your kinky hair—something, in other words, that will allow you to work *with,* instead of against, your hair. Believe me, it'll be a lot less frustrating to deal with, and I think you'll be happier!

6

SHAPE UP YOUR SHAPE!

Y OU MAY NOT BE SHAPED
like an hourglass, but that doesn't mean you can't try, does it?

Ideally, your bust and hips should measure the same, and your waistline should be ten inches smaller. Remember, that's an ideal, and because nature has given women a larger bone structure in the hip area, an hourglass figure is hard to achieve. But let's try and shoot for it anyway, okay?

GETTING THAT HOURGLASS FIGURE

The first thing you should do is get out a pencil and a piece of paper and copy down the shape-up chart on the next page. This sheet will be used to chart your progress from now on. It will give you an idea of how well—or how badly—you're doing with your shape-up program.

SHAPE-UP CHART

	DATE	DATE	DATE	DATE
Bustline				
Waistline				
Abdomen				
Hipline				
Body tone				
Backside				

Measure your bust, waist . . .

The next step is to find out what you have to work with now. So, get a tape measure and stand in front of a full-length mirror without your clothes (come on—you don't look *that* bad!). If you measure over your clothes, you're only wasting your time, because you won't get accurate measurements. And accuracy is extremely important here.

To get your *bustline* measurement, place the tape just under your bustline, on your rib-cage, snugly but not too tight, and be sure the tape is even all around, as illustrated.

Close your eyes and mark the *exact* place on the tape, look at the measurement, and add five inches to it, writing it down on the shape-up chart. Closing your eyes when you measure will help insure accuracy—it's so easy to move the tape to where you want it! You should measure your bustline this way, instead of directly over your nipple area, because the breasts change size several times each month, especially right around the time of menstruation. The five-inch allowance gives a much more accurate total.

To measure your *waistline,* bend forward, mark the point

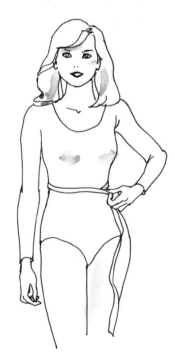

109

. . . your abdomen, and hips.

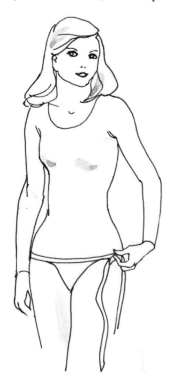

where your skin folds, stand up (making sure you keep track of that point), and that's where you'll measure. This is definitely the area where most people tend to cheat, so don't be tempted. Remember, you'd only be shortchanging yourself if you did. Close your eyes when you measure, then open them once you've marked it. Enter the measurement on your chart.

Next is your *abdomen.* This is the part that usually shares second place, with the hips, in getting out of shape fastest. Measure three inches below your waistline; place the tape there and record your measurement—again making sure you close your eyes before marking the right point. Write the results down on your chart.

To get your *hip* measurement, go down seven inches below your waistline and measure around, using the previous method. Once again, write it on your chart.

Finally, stand in front of a full-length mirror and take a good look at yourself, paying special attention to the *tone* of your body. Is it in good shape, or is it ripply and out of shape? Turn around and look at your backside, using a second mirror. Is this what you want others to see? Write your findings on the chart.

Be sure to measure and take stock of yourself weekly, adding more weeks to your chart as needed. You'd be surprised how much your body can change from week to week, so stay on top of it.

Now, take a look at your chart. How'd you do? Naturally, the areas you're not pleased with are what you want to work on. Disregard those areas that don't appear to need improvement for now.

To show you how to evaluate your own chart, I've included a sample one, with an evaluation.

110

SHAPE-UP CHART

	DATE 5/15	DATE	DATE	DATE
Bustline	33″			
Waistline	27″			
Abdomen	30″			
Hipline	36″			
Flesh	flabby thighs			
Backside	needs firming			

Most goals are based upon what you'd *like* to have; in this case, the goal is to have the bustline and hips the same size, and the waistline ten inches smaller. You can see that this person's figure is not exactly perfect, but nevertheless, it isn't too bad either. The bustline can probably be firmed up; and in the process, the size might increase a bit. Keep in mind that, other than plastic surgery or implants, there's not too much that can be done to increase the size of your bustline substantially once you're fully developed. Exercises do help firm it up a bit, though. Your best bet is to accept it and learn to play up other areas. The waistline needs to be smaller, and the upper legs and buttocks need to be firmed up, as well.

What do *your* results tell you? If you have the opposite problem with your bustline—it's too large—there are a couple of ways you can go. First of all, if you're excessively overweight, by losing weight in other parts of your body, you'll probably lose some weight in your bustline, too. However, if you're fairly proportionate otherwise but your breasts are truly too large, unfortunately, dieting or exercise won't do anything to decrease them. Their size is usually inherited. Instead, if you're bothered by it, you may want to play down that area by bringing attention away from it. Take another look at the chapter on wardrobe in the optical-illusion dressing section.

How about the rest of your body? Again, if you have the opposite problem—too small a waistline, hipline, etc.—lucky you. There are probably many people who would love to have your "problem"! However, if *you* feel too skinny, your goal then is to go on a *weight-gaining* program, making sure you select foods that are high in nutrition, as well.

Hang onto your results for now. At the end of the chapter, I'll give you some exercises that will help you get into the shape you want. First of all, however, let's talk about your eating habits.

EATING FOR BEAUTY

If you found you could stand to lose a little weight (which is most people's problem), you'll be pleased to learn that, contrary to popular belief, there *is* a slimming way to eat and enjoy your food at the same time! It's based on quality, not quantity.

In other words, many dieters become too concerned with the *quantity,* the amount of calories they consume each day, instead of the *quality,* the nutritional value, of what they eat. For this reason, I'm not going to discuss the ideal weight for you. Not only are these statistics ever-changing, but we're concerned with how the weight looks on you right now, *not* what the scale reads! (To find out what your ideal weight should be, contact a nutritionist or your family doctor. He or she knows your body and is able to advise you.)

An example of someone concentrating too much on quantity is the dieter who, after a day of counting calories and not eating enough, then happily rewards herself with a huge meal, all the while believing that she's truly sticking to her diet. After all, she starved herself all day, and she feels she deserves it! The only problem is that her huge meal is a gigantic chocolate sundae! Sound familiar?

Before discussing a diet plan, let's first go into what you should be eating, for your health and beauty.

Most importantly, *never* cut out food totally when dieting. Whether you're overweight or not, your body still needs fuel, and your body's fuel is food. Instead, eat three moderate-sized meals regularly. And if your goal is to gain weight, eat three large meals a day and supplement with in-between meal snacks.

Nutritionists generally recommend that the daily diet include foods from the four basic food groups, with a certain amount of servings from each. Two servings a day should come from the meat group. In addition to red meat (such as steak, hamburger, and pork chops) this includes poultry and fish, as well as soy beans (tofu is a good substitute). Although eating red meat on a regular basis is not recommended because of its high fat content, if you do, get the leanest meat possible. Make sure you cut off any visible fat before cooking. Broil meat instead of frying it, and blot off any excess oil with paper towels before eating it.

In addition to the meat group, two servings each day should come from the milk group. Nonfat milk is better for you, as it contains less fat. In fact, get into the good habit of drinking sweet acidophilus milk occasionally. This is milk, but with an important ingredient added—the lactobacillus acidophilus, which gives your system natural digestive aids you may not be getting, as many of today's foods are overprocessed and refined. You can find it at almost all health food and some grocery stores. It tastes just as good as "regular" milk. Plus, this kind of milk is great for people whose systems can't tolerate other kinds of milk.

Also included in this group is cheese. I'd recommend eating lowfat or nonfat cheese, particularly if you are trying to lose or maintain your weight. Also stay away from processed cheeses, whenever possible. There's usually not enough nutrition in them or any processed foods. Instead, eat unprocessed cheeses (pay attention to the label to tell you whether it is or not).

Four servings daily should be vegetables and fruits. Keep them as fresh as possible, and try to include yellow, as well as green, leafy vegetables in your diet. If you must eat canned fruit, be sure to rinse the fruit off with water in a colander, especially if you are trying to lose weight. Many canned fruits contain lots of sugar. When cooking vegetables, be sure to steam them with the lid on the pan. It's the best way to keep in nutrients, which would otherwise be lost to the air, through steam.

You should have four servings a day from the bread and cereal group. Whole-wheat bread is usually better for you, as it's unprocessed. Selecting cereals (and other foods, too) high in natural fiber or whole grains is best. Also, get into the habit of reading food labels for their ingredients. Some cereals contain what is called non-nutritious fiber, sometimes made from sawdust. Make sure your choice of cereal is low in sugar, too. It's not only fattening, but sugar has very little, if any, nutrition.

Most foods other than those grouped above are probably not only unnecessary but, usually, very low in nutrition; and you'd be better off concentrating on foods within the basic food groups instead. Called "empty foods," because of their lack of nutrition and high-calorie content, such foods usually include sugar (most foods contain enough natural supplies of sugar for your body). Garnishes such as mayonnaise, relish, mustard, and margarine or butter, in addition to oily or creamy salad dressing (lemon juice, vinegar, or pepper and other herbs taste just as good) should be avoided on a regular basis. Stay away from salt, too, as it tends to make you thirsty and consequently retain water (one teaspoon of salt retains one quart of fluid!). This certainly makes you look heavier than you are. If you must snack, eat fresh vegetables; keep to a minimum the amount of fruits you eat, as they do contain a lot of sugar. While fruit is important, it is one food that many people abuse. If you're trying to keep your weight down, you'll want to keep fruit eating under control. However, if you are trying to *gain* weight, you can afford to eat more of snack foods than many other people. Just remember to eat nutritiously, though.

Like any other change, it does take a while to adjust to a new diet. Once you give it a good try, you won't ever want to go back to junk foods as your main diet. Take it from me. I was once a junk-food addict, and if I could change, *you* can, too!

Now that you have a general idea of what you should be eating, the most important part is to put together a plan that will work for your particular needs. To do that, I'd suggest seeing your doctor, nutritionist, or dietitian first.

Once you've discussed the best plan to use, there's a great way to monitor your eating habits, especially if you're trying to lose weight or you just want to maintain your present weight. Do a "diet diary" for one week. In this diary, you will be writing down *everything* you eat for the week. Then compare it against the plan your doctor has given you, and circle the "no-no's" (foods you shouldn't be eating as well as excessive quantities). To correct your habits, start a second week's diet diary, comparing it again with the plan you were given. Do you have fewer circles?

While the plan your doctor gave you will probably work well for you, following the same food plan day in and day out might get pretty boring after a while! Plus, most diet plans are for general guidance and you will probably want to add your own personal touches to it. However, be sure to ask your doctor to guide you when selecting your own foods. He or she knows your particular needs best. And, by keeping a diet diary, you can vary the food you eat without going off the plan your doctor wants you to follow.

You may want to continue keeping this kind of diary for several weeks, circling the no-no's until you have the system down. But remember, once your diet becomes circle-free, don't think you're off the hook, because it's easy to get lazy and slip back into old habits again. Goal attainment is an everyday job without any holidays!

Another reason for consulting a professional for guidance beforehand is that many people tend to overdo a diet plan, especially those who want to lose more weight than they really should. Unfortunately, a growing number of young people, usually in their teens and twenties, suffer from a disorder known as anorexia nervosa. Much still needs to be learned about the causes of this terrible disease, but we do know that these people diet excessively, literally starving themselves. The victims of anorexia nervosa often use very thin people such as high-fashion models to imitate. But they go overboard. The result is a grossly underweight person who comes

116

close to and can actually die unless he or she begins to eat. If you know of anyone who might have this or any other eating disorder, try to persuade that person to get professional help as soon as possible. All bodies need food, and good looks are great, but not at the expense of one's health.

YOU *CAN* STAY ON A DIET!

Yes, you can! But, since the success of getting, and *staying,* in shape is based upon your own self-motivation, here are some helpful hints:

- Do nothing else but *eat* when you eat. If you're busy doing something else while you're eating, you probably won't pay enough attention to what you're doing and will eat the wrong foods, or, worse yet, you'll eat too much food.
- If you're dieting, don't eat from a large plate. Eat from a small one. It'll look like you're eating more food than you are.
- Chew everything slowly and don't gulp your food—your stomach will think it's eating more food than it is. In fact, it takes thirty minutes from the time you start eating until the brain receives the signal that it's receiving food. A fast eater can put away a lot of food in just thirty minutes!
- Never take a second helping of *anything*—at least if you are trying to keep your weight down. Remember, once again, it's quality, not quantity, and a second helping might lead to a third.
- Set your fork down between bites. You'll get so tired eating that you won't want to make a hobby of food anymore.
- Occasionally, reward yourself for good behavior by buy-

ing yourself a small gift, such as cologne, a magazine, etc. It'll make dieting much more fun. But remember, don't reward yourself with food—*that's* no reward! (Unless, of course, it's fresh vegetables!)

- If your goal is to lose weight, think slim, and you will be. Some people even paste pictures of slim and beautiful people on their refrigerator door. It helps them to "remember."

- If you have a lot of weight to lose, a good motivator is to buy an attractive outfit one size smaller than what you are. Hang it in your closet where you can see it. You'll end up wanting to wear your new outfit so much you'll start losing weight right away.

- Make eating an enjoyable activity. Garnish your food with parsley, cinnamon, or other herbs and spices to make yourself feel special. Also, take only two bites of one food, then one or two of another on your plate. Why? Because the first two to four bites of the same food have maximum taste and are the most appreciated. After that your memory kicks in and you are no longer aware of taste. So vary what order you eat your food in at mealtime. It will be a lot more enjoyable.

- And last, if all else fails, make an appointment with your doctor, nutritionist, dietitian, or someone who specializes in eating disorders. They're professionally trained to help get to the heart of the matter.

GETTING THAT BODY MOVING

Eating the right kind of food is only half the battle when you want a gorgeous figure. Your shape-up program won't be totally effective until you combine a healthy diet with a good exercise program. Even skinny people need to exercise for

118

good health, although, if that's your case, you don't want to go overboard. You want to keep the calories on, remember?

Exercise is very good for your body *and* your mind. Not only does exercise trim and firm, but it increases your body's blood circulation and gets the blood moving. It also gives you a feeling of vitality. For example, have you ever woken up feeling tired and sluggish, knowing that you have a full day ahead of you? One great way to get yourself going is by exercising. Plus, research has shown that weak and brittle bones are related to a lack of exercise.

So now you know what plain old exercising can do for you —*plenty!*

Your Personalized Exercise Program

The first thing to remember when beginning any exercise program is to start *slowly,* making sure you condition yourself. It's very important for your body and mind to get used to a consistent schedule, if they aren't already now.

I feel one of the main reasons so many people drop out of an exercise program before they even give it a good try is that they set their goals too high at first. They go into it with all the zeal in the world, doing an hour and a half of exercise every day, and in that time doing every conceivable exercise known to man. No wonder they give up—it's too much, too soon, too fast—and not very realistic!

Instead, set smaller goals, yet leave them high enough to be a challenge. After all, you'll only do as well as you challenge yourself, but if it's not big enough to work toward, you won't push to succeed.

To give you an idea of a realistic goal to work toward, think about how much exercise you've been getting in the recent past? None? Then, realistically, it's probably best to start out with fifteen minutes 2–3 times a week and build up from there. If you used to exercise regularly but haven't lately, you are probably literally starting all over, so don't try to start where you last left off. Set your goals a *bit* higher than what you've been doing and add to them as you reach that level. *That's* more realistic, and that's smart! And remember, depending upon what level you started at, it may take you some time to see any progress. In the beginning, you'll probably feel some mild discomfort, because you'll be using muscles you haven't used in a while, and your progress rate may vary —some weeks will be good, and some weeks won't be; it may even take a few *months* to see a big difference. So don't give up. Every time you exercise, you're making a little progress, and in time it will add up to a big difference. It's worth it, and you'll be very proud of yourself!

Another point to consider is how often you exercise. Of course, seven days a week is best, because our bodies respond better to regular exercise. But really, can you *stick* to a goal like that on a regular basis? For this reason, think how many days a week your body, and mind, would be willing to exercise. Three days? Four days? Schedule your exercise time on your calendar if necessary and *stick* to it.

If you find exercising dull, make it into a positive experience. Play your favorite music in the background. Reward yourself with a break during, or after, it. Dull doesn't have to be boring!

Now that you've set your goal and have a workable plan, get the shape-up chart you worked on earlier. To refresh your memory, once again check the areas you need to work on.

Whatever your problem areas are, always start with a few stretches—it'll wake you up! And always do a few conditioning exercises first. *However,* if you have a condition or injury that may be aggravated by the following exercises, be sure to check with your doctor before attempting them. Otherwise, you might injure yourself. Here are a few ideas to get you started:

With arms above your head, stand up straight and reach as high as you can above your head, keeping feet flat on floor. Be sure to tighten buttocks to prevent a swayback when stretching. Hold stretch for 5 seconds, relax, and repeat 2 more times.

Next, standing with slightly bent knees, clasp wrists in front, slowly turning shoulders from side to side a few times. Make sure movement occurs from waist up only to get full effect of stretch.

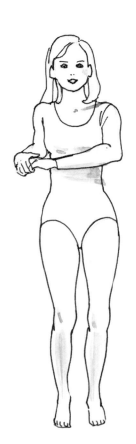

121

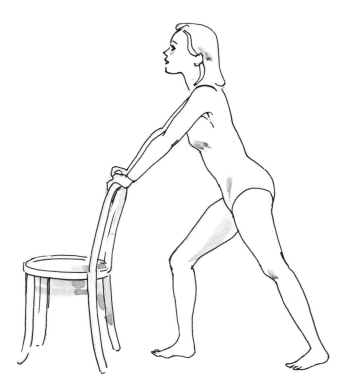

This is a great calf stretcher! Lean against a sturdy object with feet about 4 feet away. Hold buttocks under. Again, to prevent a swayback—which would decrease exercise's effectiveness—bring one of your feet forward, keeping the heel of the other foot flat on the floor. Hold this position for 5 seconds, stretch the other way, and repeat once more.

Once you've done a few stretches, gently run in place—it makes you feel terrific! Always make sure you place your heel all the way down with each step for best results and to prevent injury.

For each of the areas you need to work on, you may want to choose from the following exercises.

For firming your bustline:

Sitting down with arms crossed in front of chest, grip forearms with hands. Press hard to a count of 8, then relax. Repeat 8 times.

*Bend your elbows at shoulder level; draw elbows back **gently**, pulling toward shoulder blades. Then bring arms forward again and repeat. Do 10 times.*

123

Standing up straight, with feet apart, slowly make large circles with arms. Hold arms high at your sides, bring arms up over your head; cross them; and circle them in front of your body. Start the cycle over again. Repeat 9 more times.

124

For trimming your waistline:

Stand with knees slightly bent, feet apart, and hands extended at shoulder height. First twist to far left; then to far right—keeping feet firmly on the ground and twisting only at the waist. Twist 10 times each side.

Avoid this exercise if you have a low back condition. See your doctor for alternative ideas. *With knees slightly bent and stomach held in, place feet apart and hands on hips. Bend from your waist to the right; circle around to the left; go up and around again. Do 10 circles.*

126

Avoid this exercise if you have a low back condition. See
your doctor for alternative ideas. *Touch toes slowly with
opposite hands, making sure you line up your arm and leg exactly
and that your stomach is tucked in at all times. Lift up your arm
straight in back, keeping knees slightly bent. Do 10 toe touches
each side.*

With feet apart, stretch your body up and **slightly** to each side. You should feel your waistline stretch. Make sure you stand upright without twisting. Do 10 times each side.

For flattening your abdomen:

Keeping back flat against floor and hands under small of back, slowly raise one leg as high as you can. Lower, raise, and lower it. Do 4 more times. Repeat with other leg 5 times.

*This sit-up really works! Lying with back against floor, knees
and head up, cup head with hands. Pull yourself partway up
until you can feel it in your stomach. (Always keep tummy in.)
Hold for count of 2, go back slowly toward the floor without
touching it, and repeat 4 more times.*

129

*Sit on the floor, bend knees, and extend arms in front of you.
Raise each leg off the ground as high as you can and hold for a
count of 10, making sure you keep your stomach in and maintain
your posture. Repeat 4 times, and do the same with other leg.*

For firming your hips:

Sit on floor, extend legs, and lean back on hands. Bend left leg so that left foot is above right knee. Twist to the right side, touching left knee to floor. Reverse leg position and twist to the left, touching right knee to floor. For maximum effectiveness, make sure you keep stomach in. Do 10 twists each side.

Lie on back, extend arms at shoulder level, and bring knees up to chest. Then roll to the left, touching knees to floor; roll to the right, touching knees to floor again. Keep shoulders flat against floor and roll from the waist only. Do 10 rolls each side.

132

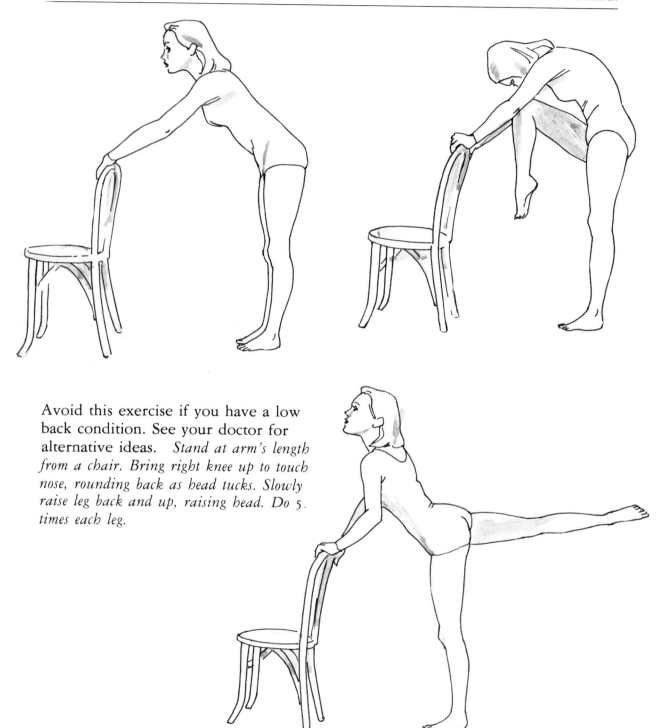

Avoid this exercise if you have a low back condition. See your doctor for alternative ideas. *Stand at arm's length from a chair. Bring right knee up to touch nose, rounding back as head tucks. Slowly raise leg back and up, raising head. Do 5 times each leg.*

For trimming your thighs:

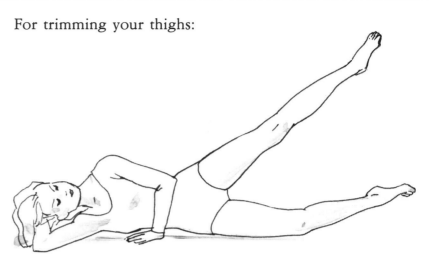

Lie on your side, with leg closest to floor bent and body straight and at a 90-degree angle to leg. Raise top leg up high, then lower it. Do 7 times each leg.

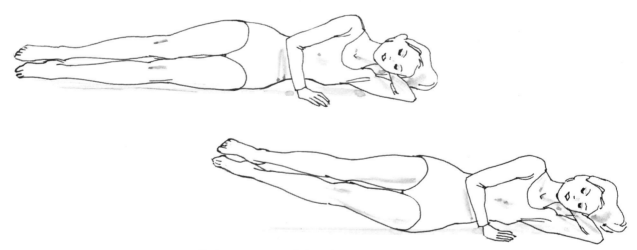

Lying on your left side, raise legs together off floor as far as possible and use your right hand for balance. Lower, relax, then repeat 9 more times on left side and 10 on right.

134

Holding a chair for support, stand with back straight, buttocks under, and stomach in. Lift right knee slowly to your side and lift leg out and back, as high as you can. Do 10 times each leg.

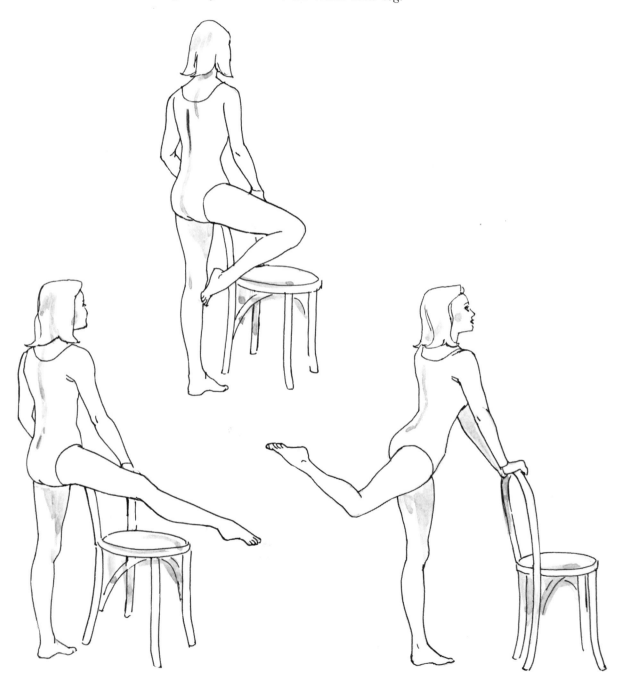

Standing with feet together and arms at your sides, rise up on toes, then lower slightly with knees bent. Strive for smoothness. Repeat 10 times.

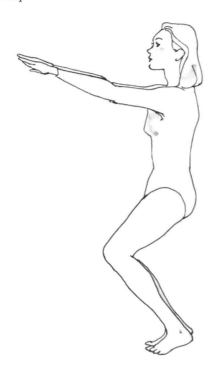

After you've mastered your original goals, be sure to add to them occasionally, but not until your *body* is ready for it. (Your mind may be ready, but be cautious—minds have a way of overplanning!) This way, you'll be building up your body's strength *gradually,* as well as getting to the goals you set for yourself.

Also remember that spot-toning won't always be enough. A vigorous cardiovascular workout is essential for continued good health. A fun way to give your heart a good workout is to do aerobic dancing. Or, if you prefer, you might like to try one or more of the following activities.

136

- Jogging, if done correctly, is a good all-round sport. To find out how to jog the right way, get one of the many jogging books on the market.
- Bicycling is fun, and great for firming your lower-leg and thigh muscles.
- Swimming is, by far, the best all-round sport. Every muscle gets a workout, and it's terrific for the back.
- Try skipping rope. It improves coordination, and it's wonderful for your shoulders and chest muscles. Plus, it can be done indoors on rainy days.
- Tennis is not only a fun, competitive sport for many, but has all-round benefits. The game also improves coordination, reflexes, agility, and balance.

The list could go on and on, but I think you have the idea by now. Outdoor activities are not only fun to do alone or with others, they are also good for you and your health. Used by themselves, they're not always effective, because weather conditions don't always allow it, so have some alternatives in mind. Whatever you do, give your body some good, regular exercise—you'll look and feel terrific!

SINCE YOU ASKED . . .

I see so much exercise equipment advertised. Is it really any good?

Oh, most definitely! Of course, exercise equipment isn't meant to take the place of outdoor exercise or sports, but it is an excellent supplement—when it rains, when you're sick and can't go outdoors, or just to vary your routine. Just make sure to get a thorough briefing from the dealer where you buy your equipment and follow directions. A lot of people have injured themselves because they didn't take a few extra minutes and read the directions beforehand!

I don't mind watching my diet most of the time, but I just love chocolate. Can't I ever have any of it? I'd just die if I couldn't!

As a fellow "chocoholic," I can certainly identify with that! Personally, I don't see anything wrong with rewarding yourself with a no-no every now and then, but make sure it's only *occasionally*. Otherwise, it becomes a habit, and there goes that beautiful figure!

How do I know how many calories I'm supposed to have per day? I've just started a diet program and am calorie counting, but I'm not sure what amount I'm supposed to have.

Determining your calorie input is dependent upon so many things: your weight goal, how soon you want to realize it, your health, etc. I can't possibly advise you with so little information. I suggest you consult with your doctor, nutritionist, or a dietitian. He or she would know your needs better.

I have just the opposite problem—I want to gain weight. I'm so skinny, everyone calls me "Toothpick." I'm not sure exactly what I'm supposed to do.

That used to be *my* nickname, too—not much fun, is it? Basically, you want to eat three large meals a day, making sure you include food from each of the four food groups. While you can use the extra calories from fat for weight-gain (assuming you have no health problems), I'm not sure you can use it for health purposes. So do watch your fat intake for the most part. Increase your serving sizes, and if you want seconds, go for it! For in-between-meal snacks, eat something fattening every now and then. Remember, while you're not going overboard and are basically eating healthily, like everyone else, you are *adding* some no-no foods to what you eat, too.

Regarding exercise, remember, to lose weight, the secret

is to *increase* your activity level and *decrease* your food intake. If you are underweight, the opposite applies to you. You're going to *decrease* your activity level and *increase* your food intake. After all that, you may find that you are still underweight. If so, consult your doctor. There may be a medical reason for your lack of weight gain. If not, eventually you may grow out of it, like I did. In fact, not too long ago, I used to eat *whole* cheesecakes at a time without gaining weight! Now even one small piece seems to go directly to my hips! So take advantage of your enviable position before it's too late.

STEP

7

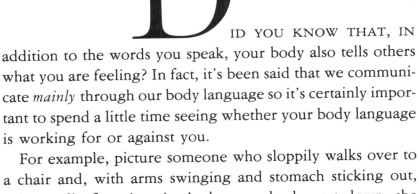

LOOK WHO'S COMING DOWN THE STREET!

D ID YOU KNOW THAT, IN addition to the words you speak, your body also tells others what you are feeling? In fact, it's been said that we communicate *mainly* through our body language so it's certainly important to spend a little time seeing whether your body language is working for or against you.

For example, picture someone who sloppily walks over to a chair and, with arms swinging and stomach sticking out, exhaustedly flops into it. And, once she has sat down, she looks like the girl here.

What is she telling you through her body? Is she confident? Does she like you or herself? Is she somebody you'd look up to?

Probably not. Even though you don't know her, you already have a pretty good picture of what type of person she is. Whether your reaction is right or not in reality, her body

140

language provided that first impression—and we rarely get a second chance to make a first impression. In fact, some human relationship experts maintain that we make an impression on another person the first *four seconds* we make contact!

Now, look at that same person again. This time, however, she's walked gracefully, but naturally, to the chair, and sat down like this girl.

It's a better first impression, isn't it? *That's* what body language is all about—looking natural, but pleasant, and making others around you feel comfortable. So, let's get to work on *your* body language. It could make a big difference, as you can see!

IS YOUR BODY LANGUAGE WORKING FOR OR AGAINST YOU?

Over the last few years, body language has become quite a science—it's called kinesics. There are lots of books out on the subject (and I'd suggest reading a few of them). In the meantime, these basic body signals and facial expressions help you communicate what you really want to "say" about yourself.

Take a look at these two illustrations:

According to kinesic experts, when you sit down, it's best to sit forward, instead of leaning backward, in your chair. Sitting forward makes you look alive, interested; sitting backward conveys, "I don't care." You don't want that!

Here's another one. It'll really come in handy, especially when you interview for a job:

Notice the person on the left. Her *ankles* are crossed; the person on the right is sitting with her *legs* crossed. Which pose gives you a positive feeling? If you said the person on the left, you're right. Crossed *ankles* usually communicate a feeling of self-control and readiness; when your *legs* are crossed, there is a feeling of unreadiness, perhaps too much self-control.

Finally, look at the following illustrations. As you can see, the person on the left has her head tilted to her right; the person on the right has her head tilted the opposite way. Generally speaking, when your head tilts to the right, you're communicating agreement; to the left, disagreement. Keep

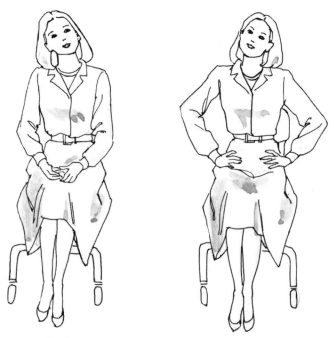

that in mind the next time you talk with your mother or father, or someone else in an authority position.

Of course, kinesics is not an exact science, because there may be *several* meanings to some of your body language. But do keep it in mind for general purposes, and as a good guide —it will really help you get along with others better, now and later on in life.

GETTING YOUR BODY LANGUAGE TO WORK FOR YOU
Learning How to Walk Again

You're probably thinking that since you learned to walk years ago, what more is there to it, right?

Actually, you're only half right, because it's not only a case of learning to walk again. It's more a case of learning *how* to walk again! Unfortunately, over the years, we tend to learn some pretty sloppy habits.

When you walk, the impression you want to give is a graceful, but natural one—a stride that spells likability and confidence, but not conceit. Of course, you're not going to be able to do all this right away. We have to do some backtracking first to correct a few things you've already learned.

So, with this in mind, the first thing to consider when walking gracefully is posture.

Unfortunately, the word posture has a bad reputation, particularly when most of us have had someone continually reminding us to stand up straight. Instead of thinking positively about posture, we tend to think that good posture is something to be avoided.

Actually, good posture is important, not only physically (it's good for your back, your internal organs, etc.) but mentally, too. It makes you look good. Also, you feel better when you stand up straight, and you'll appear confident. A wonderful side benefit of standing up straight is that visually, at least, you'll lose about one inch from your waistline and add one inch to your bustline. If *that's* not enough motivation for you, I don't know what is!

To find out how good your posture is now, here's an exercise you may want to try:

Stand up straight against a wall, with your feet about a foot away. Take your left hand and, without forcing it, slide it through the small of your back.

If you can't get your hand all, or most, of the way through, congratulations—you probably have beautiful posture! If so, skip onto the next subject, bending your knees, as there's no need to do what immediately follows.

However, if you can get your hand most of the way through, you probably have poor posture, and most likely, a swayback, too. It's rare to have perfect posture, however, so

144

if you don't, cheer up —you have plenty of company!

To correct your posture, stand a foot away from the wall. Lean against the wall without moving your feet (see first illustration) and, pretending that you're going to sit down, "travel" your back down against the wall, as in the second drawing. Then travel up against the wall with your back flat against it. Hold this position (to see the difference, try to get your hand through the small of your back now), and push off the wall with your hands (illustration three). Feel different? *That's* perfect posture!

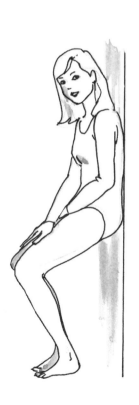
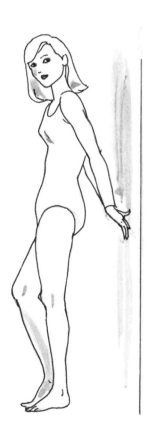

Good posture will probably feel very strange at first, but it's like anything else that's new. After some practice, it will become second nature. Give it several days of practice. After all, it probably took you several *years* to develop poor posture, so good posture won't happen overnight.

After giving it a good try, if you're still not convinced you look better, turn sideways in front of a full-length mirror and stand the way you used to, then the new way. You're bound to notice a big difference.

② The second consideration when learning how to walk gracefully is whether you bend your knees. When learning good posture and walking habits, many people tend to lock their knees.

Remember—you're after a natural look. So, when you walk, just remember to bend your knees *slightly*—it'll make you look and feel more natural.

③ The third thing to consider is whether you're a soft or hard walker. No doubt you already know, especially if you live in a two-story home and your parents are always telling you it sounds like the ceiling's going to fall through when you're walking upstairs!

To help you see the difference between a soft and a hard walker, visit a public place, such as a shopping center. Sit down, and do some people-watching. Hard walkers, whether they're overweight or not, will communicate a heavy appearance, just in their walk. They seem to move around as if they're carrying a ton of bricks. Soft walkers, on the other hand, will walk as if they're on clouds, without looking conceited or arrogant. They look controlled and self-assured. That's what you're after.

146

Now, walk naturally for a few days but pay attention to whether you're a soft or a hard walker. If you're still in doubt, ask several people whose opinion you trust. If you find out you're a soft walker, go on ahead to the fourth consideration, gait. If not, keep reading.

To turn your hard walk into a soft one, think tall when you walk, as if you are reaching toward the sky with your head, instead of slumping down toward the ground.

Another way to change your hard walk is to practice walking with a medium-weight book on your head. At first, the book will probably slide off, but eventually, you should be able to walk around without it falling off at all.

(4) The next step, when learning how to walk gracefully, has to do with the size of the step you take. Better known as gait, this is a problem most people have and is caused, among other things, by being in too much of a hurry. Mistakenly believing they'll get to their destination sooner by taking large steps, most people eventually find they don't.

Not only does taking too large of a step look bad, but you usually knock your posture out of kilter, too.

How large of a step should you take? Of course, it all depends upon your body size, but the larger you are, the larger step you're going to take.

A small-boned person would take a smaller step (about four inches apart) than a large-boned person (who takes steps about eight inches apart). If you have a medium build, you're going to take steps somewhere between four and eight inches apart.

However, don't become so concerned with inches that you are always looking at your feet. Instead, have someone watch your feet for you until you've got it down.

⑤ The next consideration is foot direction. I've seen it all . . . duck-walking, pigeon toes, you name it! So, this is definitely an area many people neglect!

When you walk, you want to keep your *heels in,* but *toes slightly out,* as shown here. Otherwise, you'll end up looking like you're waddling, instead of walking.

The reason for the angled foot is that our bodies look better at an angle rather than straight on. When reading a fashion magazine, notice how most models pose at some sort of an angle. It not only adds interest, but makes them look shapelier. You can, too!

⑥ The last thing to consider when learning how to walk gracefully is how to move your arms. Most people tend to either swing their arms too much or not enough. Also, many people have a tendency to swing their arms too far away from their body, which only brings attention to the hip area. You might as well carry a large sign reading, "Look at my hips"!

The most important thing to remember is to swing your arms from the shoulders, *not* the elbows (although it's all right to bend them slightly). To test yourself, stand sideways toward a mirror with your eyes closed. Swing your arms, paying close attention to swinging them from your shoulders. Open your eyes and see how good you look. Swinging your elbows makes you look sloppy and communicates a don't-care attitude to others. And you don't want that, do you?

To prevent yourself from swinging your arms too far away from your body, face a mirror and swing them naturally. Ideally, you want to swing your arms lightly past your garment, or hips (not bouncing them off your body). Also, when you swing your arms, make sure you don't swing more in front than in back of you. Otherwise, you'll look unbalanced.

Instead, your goal is to swing in front *and* back of you at about equal distances. A good analogy is icing a cake: When spreading the frosting, you usually spread it all over the cake, not in just one clump, right? Well, you're after the same balance here, too. It looks graceful, and you'll look terrific.

That's all there is to walking. And you thought you already knew how to, didn't you?

Going Up and Down Stairs

As with many other things, there used to be a right and a wrong way to go up and down stairs. Times have changed, however, and instead of a right or wrong way, there's a *better* way. It's simple! The only things you have to remember are to maintain good posture and to keep from bouncing. To do this, think "soft." You may want to imagine your entire body gliding on top of a cloud. Also, no matter how much of a hurry you're in, try to keep from skipping steps. That's for children at play—not you!

Standing

Just like going up and down stairs, there used to be a right way and a wrong way to stand. Today, whatever way you'd like to stand is acceptable, with one major exception: Don't point your hip out when standing. It will only put undue stress on your back, and, according to many orthopedic specialists, it might cause permanent damage to your spine. So, stand up straight!

A graceful-looking way to stand is with your feet staggered a few inches apart, toes pointed out slightly. And, unless you are holding something, make sure your arms and hands are relaxed but controlled-looking.

149

Stooping

The most common mistake I've seen made when stooping is to bend from the waistline, sticking out the rear end for all to see and putting a lot of pressure on the back. It looks ghastly.

The best way to stoop is to let your legs do the work for you. Stoop all the way down, approaching the object you want to pick up from the side. That's all there is to it.

Sitting

Here's an area that probably really needs work!

When sitting down, all that's really necessary is to approach the chair, turn, and, making sure the back of your leg gently hits the front of the chair (to prevent yourself from sitting down on the floor), drop down to the front edge of the seat. Make sure you keep your buttocks tucked in.

Once you're seated, slide yourself to the back of the chair, making sure you sit up straight at all times. Posture counts when sitting, too!

When you're ready to get up, reverse the procedure by sliding yourself to the edge of the chair and push up from the seat.

What should you do with your legs while sitting? Well, you can cross them. If you do, make sure you don't bounce the crossed leg. It makes you look nervous. Also, bring the foot that's on the floor out from under the chair a bit—this makes you look much better.

One word of caution about crossed legs: While they do look very attractive, they can provoke circulation problems, such as varicose veins, because they put too much pressure on your legs.

150

The best thing for your legs is to cross them at the ankles. To do this, simply angle your body to the left (or right, if you're left-handed), cross your legs at the ankles, and place your feet to the right (or left, if you're left-handed).

If you don't like to cross your legs or ankles and prefer to sit some other way, just make sure you don't separate your knees too much. It looks awful, especially when you're wearing a dress.

Regarding your hands, there is really no right way to place them, only a couple of wrong ways. First, don't clasp your hands too tightly together. It spells "nervousness" to anyone watching. Even if you are nervous, showing it can sometimes make you feel even more so. And, try not to change hand positions too often.

Carrying a Handbag

Here's another area where I see lots of mistakes being made, most of which communicate "I don't care."

The shoulder bag is, by far, the most popular type of handbag nowadays, so let's look at that first. When placing it on your shoulder, try to do it without swinging the bag—and possibly hitting someone standing close by. Remember, you're not a contestant in a demolition derby, and placing it gracefully on your shoulder is all that's needed. Place your fingers around the bottom portion of the front straps, not the straps themselves. It will fall to your side much nicer.

If you're carrying a lot in your shoulder bag, take turns carrying it on both shoulders. Otherwise, you may knock your good posture out of kilter, as well as put unnecessary strain on your body.

Running a close second in popularity is the clutch bag. It's not really designed to carry a lot, so if you have only a few

151

items in it, hold the top of the bag between your thumb and forefinger, trying not to clutch it too tightly; and carry it naturally down at your side.

If you've put quite a few things in it and it's heavy, carrying it between your thumb and forefinger will only make you look lopsided. So, in this case, simply tuck it under your arm. That's all there is to it!

Finally, regardless of the type of handbag you carry, try not to clutch it so close to you that you give off an ''I don't trust you'' message (even if you don't trust them!). You can hold onto your bag firmly and securely enough without looking paranoid.

Putting On and Taking Off a Jacket or Coat

When putting on a jacket or coat, take the top by the label (or where one would be, if there isn't one). Slide the garment over one arm and shoulder, then right around the bottom portion of your back. You'll automatically find the entrance to the hole for the other arm.

Putting on . . .   *and taking off a coat or jacket.*

When taking off a coat or jacket, take the garment by the lapels. Instead of pulling your coat open and showing off a possible torn lining, slide it up on top of your shoulders. Let it fall back, catch it by the label section, and place it over your arm.

153

Getting In and Out of a Car

One complaint I hear constantly from boys is how girls get into and out of cars. Believe it or not, they *do* notice! And if you watch how other girls do it, you'll find that the boys might be right!

When getting into the driver's seat of a car, try to keep your knees and ankles together. I know it's hard, but once you perfect it, it'll look much more attractive than getting in one leg at a time. The same goes for getting out of the passenger's seat, too.

To get into the frontseat: Bend your knees, leading with your fanny slightly to the side of the seat. After you're seated, bring your knees in, then your feet, and get comfortable. To get out of a car, lift your legs out of the car, twisting your body and using your arms as anchors against the seat or the dash. Then, push yourself out, making sure you don't stick your fanny out more than necessary—it's not really a very pleasant sight for your fellow passengers to look at!

When you're getting in or out of the back of a car, it's almost impossible to be poised while doing so, but do your best by thinking "graceful"; also, keep your movements as smooth as possible. And again, while you will be sticking your fanny out a bit, try to keep it to a minimum.

SINCE YOU ASKED . . .

When I walk and act poised, I feel fake. What should I do? I want to feel comfortable, but I want to look good, too.

I agree with you. If you can't feel comfortable with what you're doing, then what purpose does it serve? But remember, especially at first, if you don't practice being poised on a consistent, everyday basis, you *will* feel fake. Once you get used to it, you'll feel comfortable.

154

It seems as if I'm the only one at school who is walking gracefully. I want to look nice, but I feel very uncomfortable walking the right way, because other people stare at me when I do.

Have you ever thought that they might be staring at you out of admiration? Yes, I agree, walking correctly sometimes seems like the exception rather than the rule nowadays. But that shouldn't mean *you* shouldn't do it, does it? Where would your individuality be if you did what everyone else did all the time? Start thinking more positively about others' reactions to you; and before you know it, you'll feel more comfortable yourself. If you went backward on your self-improvement program, you'd only be hurting yourself in the long run.

When I point my toes out when I walk, I feel funny—almost like I'm walking like a duck. What do you suggest?

Well, several things come to mind. First, you may not be used to walking with your toes pointed out. If so, give it some good, consistent effort and you'll get used to it. Or, you may be pointing your toes out *too* much. Remember, you're only supposed to point them out *slightly* when you walk. Otherwise, you will look like you're waddling! The third thing that comes to mind is this: When you point your toes out, are you bringing your heels *in* at the same time?

What's the best way to carry a backpack—I don't usually carry a handbag, and I was wondering what you thought.

Very similar to a shoulder bag, actually. When putting it on your back, make sure you don't *swing* it toward others, possibly hitting them. Also remember that, just like a shoulder bag, if you put too many things in your backpack and wear it toward one side most of the time, you may knock your good posture out of kilter and put undue strain on your body. So, if possible, pack it reasonably light and carry it directly in the middle of your back. If you do carry it on your side, take turns carrying it on either side for balance.

How should I act when a boy is helping me to put on and take off a coat, or get into or out of a car? So few of them do it now that I don't know what I should do.

Let him! Yes, so few boys do those things for girls nowadays and that's a shame. In a way, I can't blame them because, along with the many wonderful things the women's movement has done for us, males are a little confused about what to do. Some women like having things done for them and some don't, so I guess the men are just playing it safe. Anyway, when a boy does offer to help you with your coat, put it on or take it off the same way you would if you were doing it yourself. But be ready to help him out a bit. If he is helping you in or out of a car, get in the same way; but when getting out, instead of pushing yourself out with your arms against the seat and dashboard, you may want to extend your hand if he has extended his, and he'll gently pull you out. If not, get out yourself. Yes, I know it may seem embarrassing to grab his hand at first, especially if you don't know him too well. However, it is a traditional custom and doesn't have to mean anything more than that!

Also, any time *anyone* helps you like this, be sure to say thank you.

DON'T
SIT
ON
YOUR
HANDS!

THAT'S RIGHT, YOU *CAN* BE proud of your hands and nails, and you don't have to hide them anymore!

Since this is a make-over book, you can't possibly avoid the subject, so, look at both of your hands and ask yourself the following questions:

1. Is the skin on my hands smooth and supple?
2. Are the lengths of my nails similar to each other or are my nails many different lengths?
3. Is the length of my nails practical for my lifestyle?
4. Are my nails clean?
5. Are my cuticles—the skin at the base of the nail—smooth or are they ragged and dry?

How'd you do? If you're not 100% pleased by your answers, then maybe it's a good thing you didn't avoid the subject, because other people *do* notice our hands, whether we like it or not!

HAVE YOU BEEN TAKING YOUR HANDS FOR GRANTED?

Before we talk about *how* to care for your hands and nails, maybe by appreciating what they're made of, you'll learn to take better care of them!

First of all, hands are very intricate in design. Did you know that there are eight wrist bones, five bones in the palm of the hand, and fourteen in the fingers, making a grand total of twenty-seven bones per hand. In fact, the bones in our hands account for more than one-fourth of the bones in our entire body.

Hands have thousands of nerve endings per square inch, which account for their sensitivity. The palm contains one of the body's richest supplies of sweat glands—one reason for clammy hands when you're nervous!

With so much to them, you should be proud of your hands. So, maybe it's time to give them some tender loving care?

HANDS THAT WORK HARD CAN STILL BE BEAUTIFUL

Of all the excuses I hear as to why many people's hands and nails look ghastly, this one is the most popular: "But I work with my hands" (cleaning, typing, etc.). That's certainly a valid explanation, but where there's a will, there's a way. It's true that working hands will never look like a hand model's, but *that's* no reason to give up entirely, is it?

158

So, here are several suggestions that will keep your hands looking beautiful, even though they do work hard.

- Don't neglect the manicure when needed. If you wait until you have time or feel like it, you'll probably never get around to it. Instead, get into a regular routine and try to do it at least once a week. By the way, be sure to do your toenails and feet regularly (called a pedicure). They count, too!

- Think of your nails as jewels, not tools. Those who use their nails as tools often wonder why their nails break. For example, when opening boxes or cans, don't use your fingernails for openers. Use *openers* for openers! Using your fingernails in this way puts a great amount of pressure on them, and since the construction of the nail has been compared to the layers of an onion, applying unneeded pressure can cause it to break.

- When washing dishes or doing other household chores, the water and detergents you use can dry out your hands, especially if you don't use any hand lotion on them afterwards. Hands are already dry, because they don't have many oil glands. Therefore, each time you immerse them in harsh detergents and water, you rob your skin of valuable moisture. What should you do? Buy an inexpensive pair of rubber gloves. It's true they're not pretty to look at, but considering the small amount of time you'd be using them, wouldn't you rather have pretty hands most of the time?

- Every night before going to bed, massage your hands (and feet, too!) with baby oil, or a comparable product. During the night, your skin will have a good chance to

159

absorb the extra moisture. Be sure to include your feet, too! If you have *really* dry skin, you may want to slather your hands with petroleum jelly and wear old cotton gloves, or plastic surgical gloves, overnight. It really works!

- You might also carry a small tube of hand lotion (unscented) in your handbag. You never know when you'll need it. Also, have a bottle of hand lotion handy wherever you think you'll need it, such as by the kitchen sink, in the bathroom, etc. If it's not close by, you may forget to moisturize when you should.

- If you have ragged cuticles, get into the good habit of pushing them back *gently*, between manicures, with a towel when you're drying your hands. Be sure to use a circular motion, and don't force them.

- During cold weather, protect your hands by wearing a good pair of gloves when you go outside. Otherwise, your hands may become very chapped.

- Most of all, practice makes perfect. Don't expect to follow the above suggestions for a couple of days then forget about them. You've got to keep it up if you want beautiful hands!

AND NOW—GETTING THOSE NAILS INTO SHAPE

Believe it or not, manicuring can be done in only five simple steps. Even better, once you have the method down, it shouldn't take you any more than thirty to forty-five minutes to do the entire procedure. And this can be done while you're doing something else.

Just as a professional cosmetologist needs the right tools to do a manicure in the salon, you will also. So, here's what you'll need:

- Hangnail nippers—an expensive item, but most have a lifetime guarantee. Hangnail nippers are so much better than biting your hangnails! Doctors don't perform surgery with their teeth, do they? So why should *you?*

Hangnail nippers.

- Emery boards—plenty of them, because they go fast. Get the long ones instead of the short tones: they're a better investment.
- Cuticle remover—in creamy form, not gel. You need to *add* moisture, remember?
- Cuticle pusher, or orangewood stick—either one will do the job.
- Nailbrush (and towel)—great for getting rid of dirt under and around your nails. Get into the habit of using your brush daily.
- Baby oil, or something comparable.
- Hand lotion, remember, the unscented kind.
- Buffing cream and buffer (optional)—great if you don't want to use nail polish, as it gives your nails a naturally shiny look. Plus, it helps smooth down any nail ridges you have.
- Cotton balls (if you use nail polish)—don't use toilet or facial tissues, because they don't absorb as well. Plus, they may disintegrate.

Cuticle pusher.

- Polish remover (if you use nail polish)—remember to buy the unscented kind. If you have really dry cuticles, get a product that's acetone-free. It usually takes longer to get the polish off but it's less dry-feeling.
- Colored or clear nail polish (optional)—try to match the

161

color family to your lipstick, if possible. There's nothing sloppier-looking than too many colors!

- Base-coat and top-coat (optional)—to be used under and over your colored nail polish. A bottom coat will help prepare a smooth surface for your polish. A top-coat will help lengthen the life of your polish.
- Nail-drying spray or oil (optional)—it quick dries your polished nails in about thirty minutes.

Now that you have the right tools assembled, let's start the manicure, shall we? By the way, the same method can be used when you pedicure your toenails. The only exception is how you shape your toenails. More on that later, on page 163.

If you are wearing nail polish, start by removing all traces of it from your nails with a cotton ball and polish remover.

Then, using your hangnail nippers, nip any hangnails you may have. Hangnails are normally little flaps of skin protruding from the sides of your nail. Remember not to force a hangnail—you'll end up tearing it and possibly inviting an infection. Also, *don't* cut your cuticles because they may grow back ragged later on. Incidentally, there are several reasons you may have hangnails—one being that you may not be moisturizing your hands enough. So, to help prevent them, make sure to slather your hands with moisturizer every opportunity you get.

Next, de-lengthen and shape your nails. When using an emery board, never file in a sawing motion—going back and forth. It will weaken your nail. Instead, file in one direction only. Find your shortest nail. Then, using the dark side of your emery board, de-lengthen your other nails to that length. I know—you don't want to do that, but nails with different lengths look tacky! Even if you have nine long nails and one

Nip all hangnails.

short one, people do notice. Besides, your nails will grow back quickly.

(A hint: While you're waiting for your nails to grow back, try some optical illusions. Just as with wardrobe and makeup, draw attention away from your short nails. Don't wear as much jewelry around your hands, for example. Instead, choose another area to play up on your body. And, if you wear nail polish, leave a slight space of uncolored nail to make shorter nails appear longer. In other words, when applying colored nail polish, don't take the color all the way to the sides of the nail. This will give an illusion of length.)

There is one exception, though. Since your thumbs are a bit farther away from the other fingers, if your thumbnails are shorter than the rest, that's fine, as long as both thumbs have nails of similar lengths.

After de-lengthening your nails, use the light side of your emery board to shape and smooth your nails into an oval. If your nails are short, file them straighter across. Be careful not to file too deeply into the corners because it weakens your nails.

File the edges downward.

Finish by filing downward on the edge of your nails, again with the light side of the emery board, to prevent snags.

When shaping your toenails, file straight across, being careful not to file into the corners, since this may provoke ingrown toenails.

Now apply cuticle remover around the bottom and side of each nail, leaving it on for a short time. Using your cuticle pusher, or orangewood stick (if you use an orangewood stick, be sure to put a thin layer of cotton on the tip), gently push the cuticle area in a circular motion.

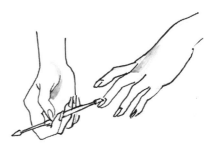

Then use the cuticle pusher.

The ideal is to have the cuticles pushed back far enough so the white "moon" shows on all nails. If yours don't show

163

at first, don't force the cuticles, because you'll tear them. Just get into the manicure habit, and before too long, you'll see your goal!

Next, using warm, soapy water, take your nailbrush and gently brush under and around each nail. It will remove any emery board fragments or dirt that you may have.

Now's the time to reward yourself, after all that work, with a massage. Squeeze a little baby oil onto your hands and feet, and gently massage it into your skin. To really moisturize, as well as seal in the moisture, slather your hands with hand lotion afterwards.

At this point, you can either leave your nails bare, polish them, or buff them.

If you'd like to wear colored nail polish, here's how to apply it: Start by applying one coat of your base-coat to your bare nails and allow it to dry for a few minutes.

Shake your colored nail polish well to blend, then rub the brush *once* along the bottle's rim to remove any excess polish. (If you rub the brush along the rim more than once, you'll find that you won't have enough polish left; not at all, too much polish left.) Apply your polish in three long strokes (down the middle and along both sides). Go up to but not onto your cuticles, if possible. If you accidentally get some polish on your cuticles, simply take a cotton swab dipped in polish remover and rub it away carefully. Wait a few more minutes and apply a second coat of colored nail polish, using the same method. Let dry.

Then apply your top-coat over your colored nail polish, followed by an application of your nail-drying spray or oil, if you use it. Just stroke it on as you do your polish. Wait between 30 and 45 minutes before you do too much with your nails, and you're all done!

164

If you prefer to use clear nail polish instead, use the same method as above, but rather than applying two coats of your clear nail polish, just apply one, because that's all you'll need.

If you'd rather not wear nail polish, you may want to use a buffing cream and buffer, instead. If so, dot a small amount of cream on each nail, and buff away.

And that's all there is to it!

Buff your nails, if you'd like.

Now that you know how to take care of your hands and nails, you'll be so proud of them you won't ever want to hide them anymore!

SINCE YOU ASKED . . .

What is the best way to prevent my nail polish from "rippling"?

The best way I can answer is to use an analogy. Before an artist can paint a picture, he or she must be assured of a smooth canvas. In the same way, you must start with a smooth surface, too. How? Remove surface soil with a nailbrush. And, be sure to remove all traces of old polish before repolishing. Also, are you applying too much polish per coat? If so, reduce the thickness of each coat.

How can I stop biting my nails? I'm trying to grow them out.

In one word—discipline! Even though there are numerous products on the market which help to prevent nail-biting, one method I've found to be very effective is this: Manicure your nails on a regular basis. Chances are that eventually you'll be so proud of your nails, you won't even *want* to bite them! An alternative method is to treat yourself to a salon manicure regularly. Many beauty colleges offer low-cost manicures. You won't feel like biting your nails, especially after spending *money* on them. And reread the hint on page 163 for making your nails appear longer while they are "growing out."

165

My fingers are short and my knuckles are large. What can I do to make them appear less so?

By creating optical illusions. Keep your nails at a longer length. Wear rings that are narrow and dainty instead of wide and eye-catching. And, when applying nail polish, don't take the polish all the way to the sides of your nail, as this will add width.

When shaping my nails, I find that the squarer shape is more practical for me instead of the oval shape. Now reading that you suggest an oval shape, should I stop wearing the square shape?

I see nothing wrong with shaping your nails in a squarer shape, provided your nail edges are smoothed over in order to prevent snags in your hosiery and other delicate fabric. Remember, though, a squarer shape is not going to look as natural as an oval one.

Every time I try to wear nail polish, I find myself peeling it off—I can't stand the way it feels. Do you think it's all right not to wear polish? I really don't even like it.

I don't like wearing it sometimes, either. If you're more comfortable not wearing nail polish, that's fine. Perhaps, to feel your most beautiful best, you may reserve wearing it for special occasions, that is, if you feel comfortable with it even then.

My nails seem to break, no matter what I do to them. What should I do?

If you have *really* tried everything, then accept them. I have the same problem with my toenails, if you can believe that— I can't seem to grow them even the least bit! I'd suggest you keep your fingernails short in length. Make sure you don't file too deeply into the sides of your nails, as you don't want to weaken your nail any further. And learn to play up other parts of your body.

Some people's nails are so long and perfect looking—how do they do it? Mine are so ugly!

While I'm sure your nails aren't really as ugly as you think they are (Are you taking care of them? Nails don't take care of themselves!), some people do have a couple of things going for them. First, and I've found that this is rare, some are born with strong nails, which don't seem to cause them any problems at all. Lucky them!

Another reason why some people have beautiful nails is that they cheat a little by wearing something like sculptured or acrylic nails. While you may be able to do it yourself at home, having it done professionally is a lot easier and insures a much more professional look. Basically, fake nails are built onto your own nails; and in a couple of hours, you have long, gorgeous nails. All that's necessary to keep them looking beautiful and staying on, other than being careful, is to go back every couple weeks or so for touch-ups. Remember, since you're not be accustomed to having nails this long, you may have to change the way you use your hands. Also, since you are having it done professionally, it can be expensive, so it really depends upon how important your nails are to you.

As far as whether or not they're safe, I've heard pros and cons. Some say that your own nails can be ruined; others say that doesn't happen. If you want to be sure, however, I'd suggest asking a dermatologist. Also, before you have it done, shop around, checking references of the salon you'd like to use.

STEP

9

IN CLOSING...

Our JOURNEY TOGETHER HAS come to an end for now, but *your* journey is just beginning! I hope this book has helped you to find out how truly special you are. Our world is a busy and crowded one, and it's too easy to get lost in the shuffle—to feel like just a nameless face.

You have so much to look forward to, and I think our experience together will help give you that confidence you'll need to achieve things you never imagined possible. Keep *The Make-Over* handy, so you can refer to it whenever you need to.

As I said when we first met, be the best you can be, and don't let anyone ever stop you from it. Keep on growing, changing, and improving. Read, study, practice, enjoy. Most important, dare to be the best *you* possible. You *are* beautiful —I really mean it!

INDEX